Jesus Against Patriarchy

The Struggle for a New Creation

Jesus Against Patriarchy

The Struggle for a New Creation

Kurt Greenhalgh

Unless otherwise noted, the Bible used in this book is the NRSV: New Revised Standard Version, Thomas Nelson Publishers, Nashville, TN, 1990.

copyright, 2024, Kurt H. Greenhalgh
Publications may use short excerpts from this book

ISBN: 979-8-218-38249-0

Published by Bradley Harper
Irondequoit, New York

Kurt Greenhalgh has written four books on the subject of radical Christianity. All four books are available as downloads directly from the website www.slaveryorliberation.org. The books are also available in traditional paperback form. The three other titles are:

Slavery and the Gospel of Liberation
Revival of the Revolutionary Discipleship Movement
Christian Idolatry/Christian Revival

TABLE OF CONTENTS

Chapter	Page
1. The World in Crisis and Why Discipleship to Jesus is the Key	1
2. Patriarchy Rules Human Civilizations	9
3. The Patriarchal Family—and Why Patriarchy is Winning on the Ground	21
4. Patriarchy and Rape Culture	41
5. Intersections Between Patriarchy, Gender, and Transgender	67
6. The Patriarchal Medical-Pharmaceutical Industry and the Drug and Alcohol Culture	86
7. Patriarchy, Genocide, and Climate Chaos	111
8. Patriarchy and Institutional Religion	139
9. The Alpha and the Omega	164

Chapter One

The World in Crisis and Why Discipleship to Jesus is the Key.

This book is all based on my own faith-perspective. What follows here is based on my personal beliefs and my worldview. Take what you will from this book, carefully consider what you will, and dismiss the rest. After all, God gave free will to humans. Essential to free will is that everyone can decide for themselves what they believe in.

So, let me share my bias, that is, my faith-perspective. What I believe is the most important thing in life can be summed up in four parts: 1. To know Jesus; 2. To love Jesus; 3. To follow Jesus; and 4. To resist Patriarchy. Jesus said, "I am the way, and the truth, and the life." (John 14:6) I believe that Jesus is basically the key to everything. I believe that Jesus is the Messiah, the Son of God, sent from God with the mission "to save the world." Maybe a better description of the mission is that Jesus' mission was and still is "to bring salvation, justice, and liberation to the whole world." This description indicates that universal liberation is the goal. And what are humanity and the world to be liberated from? In short—from the power and rule of Patriarchy. The real Jesus is totally against Patriarchy. The real Jesus is all about overcoming Patriarchy and spreading a revolutionary alternative to Patriarchy on Earth, i.e., the "kingdom of God"—or the "commonwealth of God."

Obviously, the world is not "saved." Massive human suffering all over the world and frequent human rights abuses and atrocities make it obvious that the world is far from being "saved." The goal of universal liberation also seems far-fetched and practically impossible. To better make sense of these dilemmas it can be helpful to put them into a clarifying "big picture" context.

Let me put forward a "big picture" context for addressing these problems. The conceptual framework that makes the most sense to me for understanding human civilization for the past

10,000 years or so and for understanding humanity's dire condition today is a *very broad understanding of Patriarchy.* *1

Feminists have greatly expanded our understanding of the meaning and scope of patriarchy. *2 There is a vast amount of feminist literature critiquing patriarchy. It is incredibly helpful. And yet most people have a very limited definition and understanding of patriarchy. Most people will "compartmentalize" their understanding of patriarchy, regarding it as another term for "sexism" or placing it in the category of "women's issues"—and thereby diminish its overall importance. But I use Patriarchy in a very broad way so that it essentially represents a comprehensive conceptual framework for critically analyzing any issue.

The big-picture context for every problem, issue, or topic is a very broad understanding of Patriarchy. The basic premise of Patriarchy is male dominance and female subordination, resulting in hierarchy, inequality, oppression, and violence. But Patriarchy is much more than that. Patriarchy helps to reveal how human civilizations have historically organized themselves for many millennia. Patriarchy has very deep roots in recorded history, in the development of tribalism, kingdoms, empires, and nations. It has deep roots in all the major institutions of a society. Patriarchal organization is accompanied with supporting patriarchal myths, philosophies, religions, and traditions. Patriarchy is supported by patriarchal languages and an enormous amount of male-generated (androcratic) intellectual thoughts and rationales to justify the various forms of patriarchal civilization. Patriarchy can be viewed as a "social totality," affecting everything. Patriarchy can be viewed as a power or force that transcends individuals and various entities. In its totality, Patriarchy can be viewed as a powerful force that "infects" everyone and dominates human civilizations. There are many variations of patriarchal civilization around the world. Despite their differences they are all branches of Patriarchy.

This book is relatively short. Although the essays on various topics are relatively short, they contain a fair amount of content but are by no means comprehensive. This book is intended to show the pervasiveness, depth, and power of Patriarchy, some of its harmful effects, and Jesus' strategy and practices for overcoming Patriarchy. Each of the following chapters will expand upon the power and rule of Patriarchy and how its comprehensive grip over human civilization is leading humanity down the path of "death and destruction."

What is the Problem?

First, the world is in crisis and the consequences are devastating. Second, individual and organized efforts to overcome the crisis and to change the world for the better are woefully insufficient. Third, there is a solution but far too few people are pursuing it.

Indeed, the world is currently facing multiple crises. The crises are inter-related and are some of the consequences of patriarchal civilizations and their economic exploitation of labor and resources during the fossil-fuel era. The crises include: Earth's 6th great age of mass extinctions of species (the Anthropocene Epoch); climate change/chaos; a massive migration of species toward the poles due to global warming and over-heated habitats; melting of glaciers and ice sheets; warmer oceans; rising ocean levels; acidification of lakes and oceans; endangered coral reefs; overfishing; depletion or pollution of aquifers; massive plastic pollution and spread of micro-plastics everywhere; decline of clean drinking water and groundwater; decline in wetlands; melting of permafrost; more frequent extreme weather events; loss of topsoil; growing desertification; more large dust storms; increasing deforestation; more severe forest fires and air pollution; steady increase in highly-radioactive nuclear wastes; spreading radioactive contamination; nuclear weapons proliferation and a high risk of nuclear war; massive military spending, weapons sales, and military conflicts; growing threat of killer drones & robots and uncontrolled A.I.; more authoritarian governments; more violent gangs/militias/cartels; overpopulation/over-consumption of Earth's resources; suburban sprawl; habitat loss; decline in bees and pollinators; a global pandemic; growing economic inequalities and growing number of people facing economic destitution and homelessness; a growing number of internally-displaced people and economic and environmental refugees; large social unrest against systemic racism, police brutality, and repressive authoritarian governments; more droughts and floods; more algae blooms; spread of harmful invasive species; and growing pollution, "dead zones," and fish die-offs. This incomplete list highlights some of the travail that the world is currently experiencing. These are not just problems for the distant future. These problems are happening now and, when taken collectively, show that the world is in a very real emergency situation right now. The problems are extraordinary — and the response of humanity needs to be extraordinary. But it isn't.

The crises the world is facing are tied together by the human factor, by the role played by Homo sapiens. More specifically, the crises are the result of Patriarchy. They are the result of male-dominated human civilizations all around the world. They are the result of patriarchal governance and economic development. Governments and large corporations are patriarchal institutions that are constantly driven to seek increased military power and economic wealth. They are a major cause and source of the world's deteriorating ecosystems. At best, they can offer top-down (hierarchical) reforms to mitigate some of the harm and damage being done. They can bring some relief—but can never get to the roots of the problems. They remain pillars of Patriarchy and it is, ultimately, Patriarchy which must be overcome.

<u>How Hard is it to Save the World?</u>

If a solution to the crises is to be found, and if Patriarchy is to be overcome, the solution must come from grassroots efforts. Individuals are doing lots of good works. Every individual is important. The personal is political. Everything is connected. Every small contribution is helpful. Good deeds live on, with a ripple effect. Acts of love and kindness strengthen social connections, bringing people closer together. Every day, every moment, provides an opportunity for doing some good. However, relying on individuals alone to overcome Patriarchy is a losing strategy. Individual efforts alone will not overcome the collective power of patriarchal civilizations.

Grassroots organizations are doing lots of good things. They are helping many people who otherwise would not be helped. They provide valuable services in many areas. They are doing important social justice education, organizing, and protesting. Some grassroots organizations can offer a counter-cultural rural alternative to mainstream patriarchal society. In general, grassroots organizations have the potential to develop stronger resistance to Patriarchy and do much more good than individual efforts. However, in practice, grassroots organizations' overall effectiveness, in relation to the world's collective crises, is limited by several factors. First, organizations and movements tend to focus on a single issue or a single area of concern. They are not holistic. They can appeal to a segment of the population and seek changes in a particular area of concern. But they can't grow large enough to really transform a patriarchal society. For example, even the renowned Occupy movement, which famously proclaimed, "We are the 99%," didn't really live up to their key slogan and could not sustain itself (although 0.01% of their activists are still hoping for a resurgence). Second, organizations and movements may have idealistic and/or radical beginnings along with strong rhetoric. But they tend, over time, to move toward a reformist legislative agenda, aimed at convincing the ruling class to make some adjustments. For example, the original energy and efforts to protest specific instances of police brutality and murder of Blacks, in particular, eventually weakened. The focus changed toward prosecutorial indictments, courtroom trials, and the details of possible police reforms. Third, organizations and movements arise but they often begin with a weak foundation and base. Such a movement may grow fast and create a lot of publicity—but then decline and fade away. For example, when the Arab Spring movement spread to Egypt it may have seemed destined to bring great changes. But it was based on the myths of democratic government, the false hope that the military would support it, and upon forging a superficial unity of the people. It failed badly.

    Despite all the great things that individuals and grassroots organizations are doing, they are not collectively powerful enough to solve the world's crises and overcome Patriarchy. Underestimating the collective evil being done by patriarchal civilizations around the world will not motivate people to make the lifestyle changes that are necessary. Patriarchy is winning on the ground all the time—with devastating consequences for humanity and for the world. Much more is needed.

    The problem is that it is very difficult to save the world from all of its crises. It is very difficult to change and transform the world. It is very difficult to build, sustain, and grow a movement that will overcome Patriarchy.

    What is to be done? Let me make a bold, faith-based assertion: *The only true hope for overcoming Patriarchy, saving humanity, and saving the world is through Jesus and his discipleship/liberation movement.* To say that Jesus alone is the only true hope may be technically true—but is incomplete and can be easily misunderstood. Jesus, the Messiah, the leader of God's liberation movement, handed on his mission to his disciples. "Go therefore and make disciples of all nations, baptizing them...and teaching them to obey everything that I have commanded you." (Matthew 28:19-20) The discipleship/liberation movement is partners with Jesus in the mission to overcome Patriarchy, save humanity, and save the world. Jesus is the strong foundation and groups or communities of disciples are the necessary base of the movement. God's liberation movement is a grassroots, participatory, egalitarian movement in which followers and disciples of Jesus play an essential on-the-ground role. This is the solution but far too few people are pursuing it. Jesus needs a lot more followers and disciples in order to build the movement and build a powerful alternative to Patriarchy on the ground.

If the assertion is true that the only true hope for overcoming Patriarchy, saving humanity, and saving the world is through Jesus and his discipleship/liberation movement, then there are some very important corollaries that need to be emphasized. I will proceed on the basis that the assertion is true and point out five corollaries.

First, all other hopes for overcoming Patriarchy and solving the world's many crises are false hopes. There are many false hopes. They will all fail. People often place their faith in false hopes and endeavors which actually end up strengthening Patriarchy. But, I suppose, it may be better for individuals to have false hopes than to have no hope.

Second, if God had not sent Jesus, the Messiah, then human beings, Homo sapiens, would go extinct. If God had not sent Jesus, then there would be no true hope for humanity. Thus Homo sapiens, like all their evolutionary hominid predecessors, would be on the sure path to extinction. Patriarchy is leading humanity on the path that leads to extinction and patriarchal civilizations have already travelled a long way down that path.

Third, the gospel, or Good News, of Jesus, the Messiah, leading God's liberation movement is *extremely hopeful.* Since God did send Jesus, not only won't human beings go extinct but followers of Jesus can be certain that eventually humanity and the world will be saved. Jesus began the discipleship/liberation movement and established a permanent divine-human partnership for the mission. With a divine leader/partner in Jesus, the discipleship/liberation movement has a permanent connection to God and to God's Spirit-power. Since Jesus exercises the full power of God it is impossible that Jesus would fail to accomplish the mission. Hope in Jesus and in his discipleship/liberation movement is well-placed. The hope is true, the hope is certain that eventually Patriarchy will be overcome and humanity and the world will be saved.

Fourth, there are compelling reasons to prioritize participating in Jesus' discipleship/liberation movement—which is the harbinger of God's New Creation. There are too many reasons to go into here so only a brief rationale will be made. Jesus said, "But strive first for the kingdom [or commonwealth] of God and its righteousness and all these things will be given to you as well." (Matthew 6:33) There is some urgency, there is some imperative, based on love for God, love for humanity, and love for all creation, to prioritize becoming part of the ultimate solution by participating in Jesus' movement. The turning of the tide will not occur until there is a strong bona fide discipleship/liberation movement with many, many participants.

Fifth, Jesus offers a unique path to universal liberation. It involves new practices and new relationships. Old strategies and practices that don't include Jesus are tragically neglecting the value and importance of God's Spirit-power. Only one path is centered around Jesus. There is only one divinely-led liberation movement. Since the path to true liberation is opposed to all forms of domination, oppression, and violence, Jesus calls people to "come out" of patriarchal structures, institutions, and relationships. Jesus said,
> "If you belong to the world, the world would love you as its own. Because you do not belong to the world, but I have chosen you out of the world—therefore the world hates you." (John 15:19)

Also, Jesus said,
> "As you have sent me into the world, so I have sent them into the world." (John 17:18)

In order to overcome Patriarchy people must separate themselves from the patriarchal world and then re-engage the patriarchal world as participants in Jesus' unique discipleship/liberation movement.

Unless there is a cosmic change of consciousness, lifestyles, and practices among homo sapiens, conditions on Earth will continue to worsen. Jesus' followers and disciples are meant to be the "vanguard" of a worldwide renewal movement, a veritable New Creation.

Footnotes

1. This is a practical big-picture context for the past 10,000 years or so. Of course, a bigger big-picture context includes the God of creation and infinite Spirit-power and makes Patriarchy look small in comparison to deep time, immense space, and God's power. In this bigger big-picture context Patriarchy is a temporary and transitory blotch of mal-directed nature. But, for practical purposes for understanding humanity's plight today, the big-picture context of a very broad understanding of Patriarchy is most useful.
2. I prefer to use the upper case "P" for Patriarchy because I want to highlight the power and resiliency of Patriarchy. Using the lower case "p" for patriarchy can subtly diminish the importance of patriarchy and underestimate the enduring power of patriarchy.

Chapter Two

Patriarchy Rules Human Civilizations

The big-picture context for every problem, issue, or topic is a very broad understanding of Patriarchy. The basic premise of Patriarchy is male dominance and female subordination, resulting in hierarchy, inequality, oppression, and violence. Patriarchal societies standardize and institutionalize hierarchy, inequality, oppression, and violence.

The rise of Patriarchy may have begun about 10,000 years ago—about the same time as the rise of agricultural production. The rise of agriculture allowed, in good years, for the storage of surplus agricultural production. This laid the foundation for a significant change in lifestyles and social relationships. The storage of surplus production allowed for the accumulation of wealth, labor diversification, an increase in trade with distant traders, centralization of power, and stronger social hierarchies. The wealth produced translated into the opportunity for patriarchal social, political, economic, and military hierarchies to further develop. Over a period of many thousands of years villages, cities, and empires developed, increasing social stratification and social inequalities.

> "[T]he use of outsiders captured in battle as slaves developed a permanent class of low status persons. Slavery was a key component of urbanization wherever cities formed in the ancient Near East. Slaves were integrated into the fabric of life, working in temples, fields, and various skilled activities." *1 Wes Howard-Brook

Patriarchal civilizations grew in power, social hierarchies, and inequalities.

This growth should not be considered a mark of true human progress, but rather it has been taking humanity in the wrong direction. In the Bible, the Fall of Adam and Eve was from the idyllic and mythical Garden of Eden, which provided food from fruit-bearing trees, into the oppressive world of Patriarchy. (Genesis 3:16-19) For Eve the punishment for disobedience to God is stated: "in pain you shall bring forth children, yet your desire shall be for your husband, and he shall rule over you."(v.16) A patriarchal hierarchy ensues where men are in positions of dominance and women are in positions of subordination—with husbands ruling over wives in the intimacy of heterosexual marriage relationships. The male-dominant patriarchal family becomes a key foundation for the growth and enduring power of patriarchal societies. For Adam the punishment for disobedience to God is stated: "cursed is the ground because of you; in toil you shall eat of it all the days of your life....By the sweat of your face you shall eat bread until you return to the ground." (vv. 17,19) Harmony between humans and nature is replaced with patriarchal efforts to dominate and exploit the natural environment, beginning with the hard labor of agricultural production.

From the above biblical passage it can be seen how the rise of Patriarchy brings divisions between those elements that God intended to be part of a harmonious whole. The rise of Patriarchy brings divisions between humans and God, between men and women, and between humans and nature. The divisions caused by the rise of Patriarchy are for the purpose of patriarchal domination, including replacing God's leadership with, primarily, male leaders.

Additionally, Patriarchy brings about a division between mind and body. The patriarchal mind-body dichotomy elevates the importance of the patriarchal mind (full of patriarchal reasonings, myths, religious beliefs, traditions, and social standards) which serves to rationalize and legitimize an unjust patriarchal social order. And Patriarchy can bring about divisions in the mind itself.

> "The dominant white Western male rationality has been based on linear, dichotomized thought patterns that divide reality into dualisms: one is good and the other bad, one superior and the other inferior, one should dominate and the other should be eliminated or suppressed. The biological base of these patterns is specialization in left-brain, rational functions in a way that suppresses the right-brain, relational sense." *2 Rosemary Redford Reuther

In the patriarchal mind-body dichotomy the patriarchal mind is dominant and the body is subordinated to it. The patriarchal mind objectifies and fashions the body for various patriarchal goals, e.g., for male strength, military power, or for controlling and channeling female sexuality into male heterosexual pleasure and/or procreation, gendered labor divisions, or female "beauty" (with associated issues such as restrictive girdles, dieting, eating disorders, cosmetic surgeries). The patriarchal mind-body dichotomy tends to repress and subordinate feelings and emotions, especially in men. It results in a loss of empathy, serving to detach men, in particular, but also women, from the suffering of "others"—especially those women, minorities, and foreigners who are at the bottom of patriarchal hierarchies. From these basic divisions and separations cited above, a patriarchal society arises.

Patriarchal hierarchies result in an unequal distribution of (dominative) power and resources. The most powerful people are at the top of hierarchies and the most powerless and oppressed people are at the very bottom of hierarchies. Patriarchal political and military hierarchies concentrate dominative power in the men at the top of the hierarchies. Historically, men have been the preponderant rulers in patriarchal societies, holding leadership positions as chiefs, kings, pharaohs, emperors, lords, generals, commanders, warlords, gang leaders, prime ministers, and presidents.

The unequal (dominative) power in relationships and in all hierarchies is oppressive and morally corrupting. As the saying goes, "Power corrupts and absolute power corrupts absolutely." Dominative power corrupts all who have it, both men and women. So, women who rise in a hierarchy face the same morally corrupting force as men in a hierarchy. The relatively small number of "token, indoctrinated, and assimilated" women rulers in patriarchal political hierarchies does not change the deep-rooted nature of patriarchal hierarchies. Patriarchal hierarchies are rooted in dominative power, inequality, oppression, and violence. An individual member, whether male or female, of a political or military institution is more conformed to and changed by the institution than is able, individually, to change the institution. So patriarchal hierarchies can, from time to time, have women as leaders (or figureheads). But the morally corrupting power of patriarchal hierarchies prevails. Dominative power corrupts—and dominative power is the key ingredient for building up patriarchal societies.

In the Bible, in the Old Testament, the relatively decentralized, but still very patriarchal, tribal association of Israel, asked their recognized leader Samuel for a change in governance.

> "Then all the elders of Israel gathered together and came to Samuel...and said to him...'appoint for us, then, a king to govern us, like other nations.'" (1 Samuel 8:4-5)

Israel's male elders asked Samuel for more powerful patriarchal rule, with greater centralization of (dominative) power, in the form of a male king—just like other patriarchal nations. God responded by saying to Samuel, "they have not rejected you, but they have rejected me from being king over them." (1 Samuel 8:7). Israel's male leaders are warned that a stronger patriarchal ruler will result in greater taxation, economic inequalities, oppression, slavery, and military apparatus. (vv. 10-18) But that last one, military apparatus, was why Israel's male leaders were willing to sacrifice so much. They said, "No! But we are determined to have a king over us, so that we also may be like other nations, and that our king may govern us and go out before us and fight our battles." (vv. 19-20) Israel's male leaders wanted a stronger political leader/ruler who would also be a strong military leader who would help Israel fight against their enemies. So, from the above passage we can catch a glimpse of how Patriarchy rules the nations and how even ancient Israel, through fear of enemies and desires for greater security, sought to conform more to the patriarchal political and military hierarchies of other nations.

The founding in the 18th century of a new patriarchal nation-state, the United States of America, has been mythologized and glorified to hide the truth that it is just another variation of Patriarchy. The "new" U.S. nation-state was yet another historical and patriarchal mutation of organized dominative power and organized violence. The all-male architects of the "new" nation often are reverently referred to as "our founding fathers." Many misguided Christians, who blend Patriarchy into their faith in God, have mistakenly believed that the "new" state came into being through divine guidance, was imbued with Christian values, and was blessed with a God-given "manifest destiny" leading to "American exceptionalism" among the nations. The all-male founders divided up the dominative power of the state into executive, congressional, and judicial branches of government, forming three patriarchal federal hierarchies. Like ancient Israel above, the top political leader, the President, was also made the top military leader, the Commander-in-Chief of the Armed Forces.

The so-called "founding fathers" of the U.S.A. were not only all-male; they were also all-white. The United States of America was founded on white supremacy and Black slavery. The U.S. Constitution legally protected the slave trade and the importation of Black slaves for twenty years. (Article 1, Section 9) The U.S. Constitution said each state could boost their population count by counting Black slaves, who had no legal rights, as three-fifths persons. (Article 1, Section 2) The U.S. Constitution also required each state to deliver escaped Black slaves to their so-called "rightful" white owners. (Article 4, Section 2) U.S. territorial expansion was founded on white-settler colonialism, displacement of Native American tribes, covetous land annexation, aggressive wars, and many policies which collectively amounted to a form of genocide against Native Americans. Thus the formation in the 18th century of the "new" nation-state, the United States of America, bears the ignominy of tying together Patriarchy, white supremacy, Black slavery, and Native American genocide.

It is noteworthy that some protests this century have targeted the removal of the Confederate flag from public places. The Confederate flag, adopted by the secessionist Southern slave states before the Civil War, has remained a symbol of white supremacy and racism. However, there has not been any comparable protests against the original American flag of white supremacy and Black slavery—the U.S. flag. This despite the fact that the U.S. has always institutionalized white supremacy and some racist form of slavery. When the 13th Amendment to the Constitution was ratified in 1865 it ended chattel slavery but allowed for "state slavery" in the form of people convicted of a crime. Racist state slavery became the norm and continues to this day through the racist and criminal legal system which disproportionately imprisons large numbers of people of color.

There are many nations in the world, with different forms of government and different cultural traditions. They reflect the many variations of Patriarchy. Patriarchy can evolve, change, and adapt—without losing its essential patriarchal nature. In the Bible, in the Old Testament, ancient Israel tried to be different from the other nations. Yet its essential patriarchal nature didn't allow it to be much different. Three millennia later the U.S.A. presents itself with a facade of trying to be different, and better, than other nations. But the U.S. has always had deep roots in

Patriarchy which has kept it on the worldwide patriarchal path of "death and destruction." Basically, despite many variations among the nations, Patriarchy continues to rule human civilizations all around the world. Even with numerous beneficial reforms, Patriarchy continues to metamorphose and adapt.

The rule of Patriarchy is very harmful. Particular attention must be given to harm done against women and girls. Under the rule of Patriarchy there is a constant, ongoing, never-ending global pandemic of violence against women and girls, in particular. There is also great violence against men and boys and great harm to the environment. But the nature of Patriarchy is such that males are the greatest perpetrators of violence and women and girls are far more likely to be victims of violence rather than perpetrators of violence. It would be naive to think that any nation or region is safe from patriarchal violence against women.

> "Rather, in all societies, women and girls are subjected to forms of physical, sexual and psychological abuse. Violence against women is carefully identified as a manifestation of the historically unequal power relations between women and men, a process which cuts across lines of income, class, and culture....Reports from the United Nations draw their conclusion: 'Gender-based violence is perhaps the most widespread and socially tolerated of human rights violations'....Virtually every minute of every day, there are incidents, somewhere, of domestic abuse, rape, honour killings, sexual violence, harassment, acid attacks, bride burning, femicide, mutilation or violation of trafficked women....The high incidence of violence against women in armed conflict, particularly where rape is used as a weapon of war, is now very evident." *3 Elaine Storkey

While violence against women and girls is pervasive everywhere, patriarchal cultures vary and some forms of patriarchal violence are concentrated in particular regions. Female femicide through foeticide and infanticide occurs because many patriarchal cultures place a much higher value on the birth of sons.

> "Gender discrimination begins early. Modern diagnostic tools for pregnancy have made it possible to determine a child's sex in the earliest phase. Where there is a clear economic or cultural preference for sons, the misuse of

> these techniques can facilitate female foeticide....census data reveal an unusually high proportion of male births and male children under five in Asia, notably in China and India, suggesting sex-selective foeticide and infanticide in the world's two most populous countries." *4

Infanticide can occur through simply "disposing" of female babies or through favoring sons and depriving girl infants of necessary food or medical care, contributing to their early deaths. Census data from India shows that the problem of female foeticide and infanticide has actually been getting worse.

> "[The Indian census] publishes the child sex ratios—the ratio of girls per thousand boys under the age of seven. Yet even these figures point to a deteriorating situation. Figures for females to males under seven from the last four census surveys show rapidly increasing disparities. The 1981 census figure was 962 girls to 1,000 boys; in 1991 this had dropped to 945; in 2001 it was only 927, and in the 2011 census the ratio had decreased further, to 914....What is clear is that the declining sex ratio cannot be simply viewed as a medical or legal issue. K.S. Jacob sees it as very firmly embedded within the social construction of patriarchy and reinforced by tradition, culture, and religion....Affluence has not challenged foeticide. It has simply made it easier." *5 Elaine Storkey

The declining sex ratio of girls to boys in India has occurred during a time where India has experienced significant economic growth. But the economic growth has not significantly changed the deep-rooted patriarchal culture.

In India the patriarchal tradition of a bride's family paying a dowry to the bridegroom's family remains very strong. Thus families with girls are economically disadvantaged and burdened.

> "In extreme cases, the newly wed bride can be murdered by her in-laws or driven to commit suicide because their dowry demands have not been fully met. In 2014, 8,455 dowry deaths were reported." *6 Elaine Storkey

When male in-laws murder newly wed brides they usually do not face any legal consequences.

Another patriarchal tradition is the so-called "honor killing" of a female by her male family members or relatives. The female victim is blamed for being guilty of "shaming" her family. The tradition is based on patriarchal family "purity codes" and strict male control over and regulation of female behavior. The practice is most common in the Middle East and South Asia, but occurs all over.

> "When so much of it occurs in countries where brutal practices exist in the dark shadows of kinship cultures, hidden in family structures away from the public gaze, these killings are insidiously absorbed within the society and slow to hit the global headlines. Yet, behind closed doors, horrifying 'punishments' have, for many years, been meted out on girls who fall foul of family traditions, or want to live like their peers. In more rare cases it has been enacted against sons also....In Pakistan...honour killing...is suspected to be the cause of death for up to 10,000 women each year, but official records account for less than a tenth of these figures." *7 Elaine Storkey

In Pakistan, as in many nations, violence against women does not get much publicity.

> "'The epidemic of sexual crimes and violence against women in Pakistan is a silent epidemic,' [prominent rights activist Tahira] Abdullah said. 'No one sees it. No one is talking about it'....Many of the attacks in Pakistan are so-called honor killings, in which the perpetrator is a brother, father or male relative....In 2020, Pakistan was near the bottom of the World Economic Forum's global gender index, coming in at 153 of 156 countries, ahead of only Iraq, Yemen, and Afghanistan." *8 Kathy Gannon

Most of the men who commit "honor killings" do not face any legal consequences.

Another strong, ongoing patriarchal tradition is female genital mutilation/cutting (FGM/C).

> "At least 200 million women and girls, aged 15-49 years, have undergone female genital mutilation in 31 countries where the practice is concentrated. Half of these countries are in West Africa." *9 UN Women

The practice of FGM afflicts a very large number of women and girls, resulting in a great deal of pain and suffering.

> "Female genital mutilation has no known health benefits, in any of its forms. On the contrary, it is known to be harmful to girls and women in many ways and is extremely painful and traumatic....Three main forms of FGM are practiced. The least invasive form, 'clitoridectomy'... involves the removal of the hood and part of the clitoris. 'Excision' involves the removal of the clitoris and adjacent labia, while 'infibulation'...is the most extensive form of

> cutting away and stitching, removing much of the tissue in the genital area....Infection, excessive bleeding, septic shock and difficulty in passing urine are common immediate effects; scarring, excruciating intercourse, kidney impairment, infertility, fistulas, and almost unbearable pain are subsequent problems. Many girls die in the aftermath of the procedure....Women are in charge of the procedures of circumcision....Yet...at a deeper level they are not the ones in control. Effectively, these women are upholding the assumptions of patriarchal authority: maintaining its powerful command over female sexuality and fertility." *10 Elaine Storkey

FGM is inflicted on girls for the sake of men. It is an example of the patriarchal mind-body dichotomy. The "patriarchal mind" is dominant and the female body is objectified, assaulted, and reconstructed for patriarchal purposes. FGM is intended to bludgeon and curtail the female sex drive, keep girls chaste and "pure" by maintaining their virginity, and prepare them for sexual domination by their future husband. Female complicity in this patriarchal practice is strong—but really reveals the deep level of subjugation of women to men and the deep level of dominance of the "patriarchal mind."

Girls and women in Indonesia, along with Egypt and Ethiopia, make up about half of the 200 million girls and women who are victims of FGM. Indonesia was briefly in the news concerning another patriarchal practice. In August of 2021 the Indonesian army became the first branch of their armed forces to announce they will discontinue subjecting female recruits to mandatory vaginal exams. This exam is also known as a so-called "virginity test."

> "During the test, a doctor inserts two fingers into a woman's vagina, based on the incorrect notion that it's possible to determine in that way whether a woman has had sexual intercourse....' 'Virginity testing' reinforces stereotyped notions of female sexuality and gender inequality,' the World Health Organization and two other arms of the United Nations said in a joint statement in 2018. 'The examination can be painful, humiliating and traumatic.' Andreas Harsono, a researcher for Human Rights Watch who has interviewed dozens of women subjected to the tests, said they described a traumatic experience, most often involving a male doctor and two nurses to hold the woman's shoulders and legs. 'It is

> sexual abuse,' he said. 'It is sexual violence.'....The tests still happen in other countries." *11 Daniel Victor, Muktita Suhartono, Christine Hauser

For female recruits the so-called "virginity test" represents a rough initiation into patriarchal military culture.

Another patriarchal form of violence against women are "acid attacks." Although small in number they do have a patriarchal character.

> "Dousing someone in acid means wanting to dissolve a person physically and psychologically. It is always premeditated, according to the United Nations....Children and men are among victims of acid attacks, but 80% are women, according to the Acid Survivors Trust International. The agency documents about 1,500 acid attacks per year." *12 Maria Versace, Ginnette Riquelme

The vast majority of perpetrators of acid attacks are men. Acid attacks are a cruel and brutal way for a perpetrator to demonstrate dominance and power over a victim. They reveal hatred and a complete lack of empathy for the victim. In a patriarchal culture that places a high value on female appearance an acid attack is intended to inflict great physical and emotional pain by permanently disfiguring a woman. The disfigurement can lower a woman's self-image and self-esteem and permanently alter how a patriarchal society sees and treats a woman.

There are other pervasive forms of violence against women and girls that will be discussed in the following chapters. The few examples in this chapter are intended to show a little bit of the deep-rooted nature of Patriarchy around the world. Patriarchy rules human civilizations around the world, without exceptions. The human costs are extremely high—as well as the costs to ecosystems and other species.

<u>Jesus and the Discipleship/Liberation Movement</u>

Assisted by their obedient soldiers, patriarchal male political and religious leaders arrested, tortured, and murdered Jesus. Jesus knows what it is like to be violated, abused, and killed by patriarchal forces. Jesus closely identifies with all people who are violated, abused, and killed by patriarchal forces. Each and every violation is a desecration of God and God's will for humanity.

Jesus' resurrection meant that God was not going to let Patriarchy have the last word. Jesus' resurrection means that Jesus/God is totally against Patriarchy and that God's Spirit-power is far greater than the dominative power and violence of patriarchal societies. In light of Jesus/God being *totally* against Patriarchy, Jesus represents the only legitimate authority to which people should deeply commit themselves.

Patriarchal human civilizations do have tremendous "captivating power" which keeps people bound to patriarchal cultures and societies. All people are immersed in patriarchal cultures and societies from their births. All people, with lots of variations, develop a patriarchal mindset while growing up. The patriarchal mindset predominates society. Most people do not see and understand how extensive Patriarchy is and end up living and perhaps trying to make small reforms within the confines of a patriarchal society. And while reforms, in the short run, can help many people, in the long run they only marginally re-shape Patriarchy. Reforms can only offer false hopes for overcoming Patriarchy. In fact, many reforms end up strengthening Patriarchy by bringing people "back into the fold," i.e., back into the mass of people who believe in and support the major patriarchal institutions of a nation.

Jesus calls people to "come out" of Patriarchy and to become participants in his discipleship/liberation movement. Part of the change people are called to make is to "change their minds" and to think more "outside the box." The Greek word, *metanoia,* often translated as "repent" or "repentance," also can mean "change of mind." To put on the "mind of Christ" means becoming immersed in a Messiah-centered reality which runs completely counter to the values and beliefs of a patriarchal society. Back in the first century the apostle Paul wrote:
> "Do not be conformed to this world, but be transformed by the renewing of your minds, so that you may discern what is the will of God—what is good and acceptable and perfect." (Romans 12:2)

Paul also wrote:
> "Yet among the mature we do speak wisdom, though it is not a wisdom of this age or of the rulers of this age, who are doomed to perish. But we speak God's wisdom, secret and hidden, which God decreed before the ages for our glory. None of the rulers of this age understood this; for if they had, they would not have crucified the Lord of

glory....But we have the mind of Christ." (1 Corinthians 2:6-8,16b)

To "come out" of Patriarchy necessitates a change from the "patriarchal mind" to the "mind of Christ." The change from the patriarchal mind to the mind of Christ is a major step toward the creation of a "new man" and a "new woman." Human beings, especially followers and disciples of Jesus, are meant to be leaders in transforming the Earth into a New Creation.

To further understand what it means to "come out" of Patriarchy it is helpful to see how extensive and all-encompassing Patriarchy is.

Footnotes

1. Wes Howard-Brook, "Come Out, My People!" God's Call out of Empire in the Bible and Beyond, Orbis Books, Maryknoll, New York, 2010, p. 41.
2. Rosemary Radford Ruether, SEXISM AND GOD-TALK Towards a Feminist Theology, Beacon Press, Boston, 1983, p. 89.
3. Elaine Storkey, SCARS ACROSS HUMANITY Understanding and overcoming violence Against women, IVP Academic, Downers Grove, Illinois, 2018, pp. 6-7.
4. The State of the World's Children 2007, ?UNICEF.
5. Elaine Storkey, pp.25-26.
6. Elaine Storkey, p. 24.
7. Elaine Storkey, p. 64.
8. Kathy Gannon, Associated Press (AP), "Pakistani women suffer in 'silent epidemic' of abuse," Star Tribune, August 1, 2021.
9. UN Women, UN, Department of Economic and Social Affairs Statistics Division, 2020.
10. Elaine Storkey, pp.31,34-35.
11. Daniel Victor, Muktita Suhartono, Christine Hauser, NY Times, "Indonesia ends army 'virginity test'," Star Tribune, August 12, 2021.
12. Maria Verza, Ginnette Riquelme, AP, "Scarred acid attack survivors seek to be seen, finally heard," Star Tribune, August 8, 2021.

Chapter Three

The Patriarchal Family—and Why Patriarchy is Winning On the Ground

The big-picture context for every problem, issue, or topic is a very broad understanding of Patriarchy. The basic premise of Patriarchy is male dominance and female subordination, resulting in hierarchy, inequality, oppression, and violence. Patriarchal societies standardize and institutionalize hierarchy, inequality, oppression, and violence. Patriarchal societies are leading humanity down "the path of death and destruction"—which ultimately can lead to extinction.

This chapter will emphasize "the patriarchal family" while the next chapter will elaborate on "patriarchal rape culture." The topics are closely related and overlap in many areas. But because there is so much to cover it is better to separate them into two chapters.

The male-dominant patriarchal family is perhaps the most important foundation for supporting and sustaining patriarchal societies. The patriarchal family is the key building block upon which other patriarchal institutions can build upon and spread out from. The extremely resilient and enduring power of Patriarchy cannot be seriously challenged, much less overcome, by any social justice movement that does not directly challenge and offer a real alternative to the patriarchal family. So this chapter will delve into the prevalence and power of the patriarchal family and why Patriarchy continues to "win on the ground" despite any number of social justice movements. And then the chapter will end by looking at why Jesus' discipleship/liberation movement is the perfect antidote and alternative to the patriarchal family.

The most basic foundation of Patriarchy is the patriarchal family. It starts in the home. "[T]he family system is the primary socializing mechanism for both personal identity *and* political norms." *1 Beginning with their births, everyone is immersed in a patriarchal culture and society. People form and develop a patriarchal family identity through patriarchal family bloodlines and lineages, strongly reinforced patriarchal family, social, and religious traditions, patriarchal heterosexual weddings and marriages, patriarchal surnames (where the wife adopts the last name of her husband), and patriarchal inheritances.

It is helpful to understand some of the origins and early traditions of Patriarchy. Much of ancient patriarchal traditions are still relevant today somewhere in the world. Many patriarchal values, beliefs, and attitudes today can be traced back to ancient Patriarchy.

The Patriarchal Family's Entrenchment in the Bible

In regard to ancient Patriarchy, the Bible is a very valuable resource and many examples from ancient Hebrew society can help to illustrate the patriarchal family. In the Bible, "the Fall" of Adam and Eve was from a state of innocence and equality in the mythical Garden of Eden into the oppressive world of Patriarchy. (Genesis 3:16-19) Adam and Eve "fell" away from God's will and into a patriarchal, heterosexual, marriage relationship characterized by male dominance and female subordination. The depth of women's oppression is revealed: its roots extend into the institutions of marriage and family. The patriarchal culture emphasizes the importance of women entering into a heterosexual marriage and the forming of a patriarchal family:

> "Yet your desire shall be for your husband, and he shall rule over you." (Genesis 3:16)

A patriarchal heterosexual marriage relationship established the man (or the patriarch) as "head" of the household (or family). The man, or the patriarch, had authority over his household. He had authority over his wife, children, servants, and possessions.

Childbearing and child-raising for a husband (or patriarch) came to define a woman's primary function and identity in ancient patriarchal societies (and in many nations today). Just as a patriarchal marriage brought inequality between a husband and wife, so child-raising brought inequality between boys and girls. According to ancient patriarchal family lineage, power and wealth passed as an inheritance from fathers to sons. Among the sons of a patriarch (or husband) the firstborn male was entitled to special birthrights.

"If a man has two wives, one of them loved and the other disliked, and if both the loved and the disliked have borne him sons, the firstborn being the son of the one who is disliked, then on the day when he wills his possessions to his sons, he is not permitted to treat the son of the loved as the firstborn in preference to the son of the disliked, who is the firstborn. He must acknowledge as firstborn the son of the one who is disliked, giving him a double portion of all that he has; since he is the first issue of his virility, the right of the firstborn is his." (Deuteronomy 21:15-17)

This passage, like so many others, has thick layers of Patriarchy. Of course, patriarchal laws favor males over females. And male privileges are codified in many patriarchal laws. But inequality is set into the above law even among sons of a patriarch (or husband)—in the form of a first-born son's birthright inheritance being a "double portion," i.e., twice as much as other sons.

The economics of patriarchal family lineages meant that investments into raising girls were for another family's benefit while raising sons was for one's own family heritage and for the parents' welfare in old age. Thus, the birth of a girl was often viewed as disappointing. Worse still, misogyny, in the form of infanticide, the abandoning of female infants, was (and still is) practiced in some nations. But the birth of a boy was seen as a blessing. Thus Eve remarks on the birth of Cain, "I have produced a man with the help of the LORD." (Genesis 4:1) Sarai (Sarah), in her desperation to provide male heirs for her husband Abram (Abraham), gave him the Egyptian slave Hagar with the hope that she would bear him a son. However, Hagar's pregnancy enhanced her status and Sarai became very jealous. (Genesis 16) The story illustrates how patriarchal values can divide women against each other and also that while women, as a class, are oppressed, women can still differ in class status—and thus experience much different degrees of privilege and oppression.

After getting married a woman's identity was submerged into that of her husband and his patriarchal family lineage. A wife could marginally enhance her status in the patriarchal society by bearing sons; she could bear a social stigma if she was childless. Labeled as "barren," patriarchal society's reproach fell on the woman and not her husband when she "failed" to bear children. Thus Rachel, Jacob's second wife, said after finally bearing a son,

"God has taken away my reproach." (Genesis 30:23) Sadly, Rachel died while giving birth to her second son—which ultimately was not really a blessing for her. (Genesis 35:16-19)

While childbearing for her husband was a woman's primary role, it was a very subservient role as the ancient biblical law makes clear:
> "When brothers reside together, and one of them dies and has no son, the wife of the deceased shall not be married outside the family to a stranger. Her husband's brother shall go in to her, taking her in marriage, and performing the duty of a husband's brother to her, and the firstborn whom she bears shall succeed to the name of the deceased brother, so that his name may not be blotted out of Israel." (Deuteronomy 25:5-6)

The main purpose of this law was to perpetuate the name and patriarchal family lineage of the sonless, deceased husband. The sonless widow found herself in a position of family limbo: unsupported, powerless, and dependent upon the decisions of her husband's brothers. They were forbidden to pass her on in marriage to a stranger. A brother of the deceased, regardless of how many wives he already had, was required to take her as a "secondhand wife" and try to impregnate her and get her to bear a son to carry on the lineage of the deceased.

One reason the patriarchal family was easy to perpetuate was because the family system upholding male dominance was self-reinforcing. Both boys and girls internalize patriarchal values as children growing up in a patriarchal family culture and society. Girls and women often have been raised and kept under male control for their entire lives (and still are today in many nations).

Girls were part of a patriarchal household, under the control and "protection" of their father. What was especially important for a father to protect was his daughters' "sexual purity." It was the responsibility of a father to guarantee his daughter's virginity for her future husband.
> "Do not profane your daughter by making her a prostitute, that the land not become prostituted and full of depravity." (Leviticus 19:29)

By maintaining girls' virginity, a father could give a daughter to her future husband and she could bear "legitimate" offspring, especially sons, to build up her husband's patriarchal family and lineage. By limiting a woman's sexual activity to one man, her husband, the husband was assured that the woman's children came through his "seed" and belonged to his family.

A newly married man had a lot of leverage/power over his new wife and could use fear as a mechanism for dominance. A newly married man could accuse his new wife of not being a virgin and unless she could prove otherwise her life was over.

> "If, however, this charge is true, that evidence of the young woman's virginity was not found, then they shall bring the young woman out to the entrance of her father's house and the men of her town shall stone her to death, because she committed a disgraceful act in Israel by prostituting herself in her father's house." (Deuteronomy 22:20-21)

A husband, if he suspected his wife of adultery but had no evidence, could accuse her, bring her before a male priest, and subject her to a priestly "test."

> "This is the law in cases of jealousy, when a wife, while under her husband's authority, goes astray and defiles herself, or when a spirit of jealousy comes on a man and he is jealous of his wife; then he shall set the woman before the LORD, and the priest shall apply this entire law to her. The man shall be free from iniquity, but the woman shall bear her iniquity." (Numbers 5:29-31)

Again, the above passages and laws have thick layers of Patriarchy and uphold male dominance and female subordination in the patriarchal family.

Only men had the authority to get a divorce—and it was a simple matter to do so.

> "Suppose a man enters into marriage with a woman, but she does not please him because he finds something objectionable about her, and so he writes her a certificate of divorce, puts it in her hand, and sends her out of his house..." (Deuteronomy 24:1)

A divorced woman would be socially stigmatized and, unless her family or someone else took her in, homeless and destitute.

The traditional heterosexual patriarchal family supports a male "head of household." This is implicitly based on an assumed "superiority" of a man and an assumed "inferiority" of a woman. Male dominance is enhanced to the extent that girls and women internalize the patriarchal belief of male superiority and female inferiority and, consequently, accept the distorted gender role and identity that a patriarchal society offers them. All the hierarchical, patriarchal institutions in a society reinforce this belief.

Ancient Israelite religion and law greatly reinforced the belief of male superiority and female inferiority. Israelite religion conveyed the notion that all bodily emissions (blood, pus, semen, excrement), as potential or real signs of sickness, decay, or death, were "unclean" and a source of "pollution."

> "Excrement is related to death. Later on, in Judaism, Gehenna, the place where offal was burned, became the metaphor for hell, that is, for the place of eternal death."
> *2 Fernando Belo

Bodily emissions made people relatively more "impure." Israel's "purity and pollution system" regarded women as naturally impure, inferior, carnal, and unfit for the priesthood. Menstruation, sexual intercourse, and childbirth were all causes of "uncleanness" which required periods of "purification."

> "When a woman has a discharge of blood that is her regular discharge from her body, she shall be in her impurity for seven days, and whoever touches her shall be unclean until the evening. Everything upon which she lies during her impurity shall be unclean; everything also upon which she sits shall be unclean....If she is cleansed of her discharge, she shall count seven days, and after that she shall be clean. On the eighth day she shall take two turtledoves or two pigeons and bring them to the priest to the entrance of the tent of meeting. The priest shall offer one for a sin offering and the other for a burnt offering; and the priest shall make atonement on her behalf before the LORD for her unclean discharge." (Leviticus 15:19-20,28-30)

With the onset of puberty and menstruation girls/women were socialized to view their bodies as "dirty"—as unclean, shameful, and contagious. Female inferiority was reinforced by requirements that females isolate themselves for much of the time because of their "contagious impurity." And female inferiority was further reinforced by the power of religious law—which supposedly came from God—and required girls/women to bring offerings to the all-male priesthood who would "make atonement" for their "uncleanness."

A similar religious law covers women after childbirth. The bodily emissions from childbirth supposedly rendered a mother "unclean" for either 40 days, if it was a male baby, or 80 days, if it was a female baby. (Leviticus 12:2-5) Afterwards, the mother was required to bring offerings to a male priest for "atonement." These religious laws became recorded in so-called "holy scripture" (the Jewish Torah and Christian Old Testament). Many people back then, and large numbers of people still today, believed that the patriarchal religious laws recorded in scripture actually came from God. They believe(d) that the patriarchal biases in scripture, in various ways, reflect God's "natural order" —rather than the human order that God is working to abolish. Of course, patriarchal religious laws and teachings support the patriarchal family and function to keep girls and women "in their place"—of subjugation to men.

Pervasive Social Support for the Patriarchal Family

Male dominance in the heterosexual patriarchal family and in society has been traditionally backed up and supported by religion, philosophy, education, laws, traditions, and patriarchal institutions. Patriarchy, for millennia, has been supported by legal discrimination against women. But to maintain such a high level of male domination over females all over the world requires more. It requires female and male internalization of patriarchal values and gender roles as well as high levels of male coercion and violence.

Patriarchy is able to sustain itself through massive amounts of family, social, and institutional education and conditioning. Everyone is immersed in patriarchal culture and society from their births. Basically, people, young and old, have only known and experienced patriarchal culture and society. Patriarchal education and conditioning form people's understanding of a so-called "natural order" and understanding of patriarchal gender roles. In general, girls and women are socialized to internalize their oppression, to be silent about their victimization, to repress their true selves in order to conform and fit in better in a patriarchal society, to identify with men, to please men, to defer to male authority and power, to turn to men for protection, to conform to feminine standards of dress, beauty, and behavior, to be nice and polite and quiet, to put their energy into domestic work, child-raising, and second-tier jobs, and to seek, when allowed, to be assimilated into patriarchal institutions.

The patriarchal order benefits from self-policing and peer pressure among females to conform to patriarchal gender roles and norms. Even so, stronger coercive methods are used in massive amounts.

Child marriage is still common today and represents one practice, among many, which strongly supports the patriarchal family. A child marriage occurs when a man marries a girl under the age of 18.

> "In 2019, one in five women, aged 20-24 years, were married before the age of 18....Child marriage often results in early pregnancy and social isolation, interrupts schooling, and increases a girl's risk of experiencing domestic violence." *3 UN Women

This is a practice that is still very strong in the 21st century and could continue to grow.

> "Worldwide, an estimated 12 million girls are wed every year before the age of 18. UN experts have predicted the [COVID-19] pandemic could lead to an extra 13 million child marriages over the next decade....Of particular concern are an estimated 30 million children who may never return to school despite lockdowns ending....'Many...are adolescent girls for whom being in school is the best defense against forced marriage and the best hope for a life of expanded opportunity.'" *4 Emma Batha

The highest rates of child marriages are in African or Asian countries.

> "A third of all girls there are married under 18 and one in seven under 15; some 'brides' are as young as five years old. But the country with the highest prevalence of child marriage in the world is Niger, where a staggering 75 per cent of all girls marry under 18, and 33 per cent under 15. This is followed by Chad and Central African Republic (68 per cent), Guinea (63 per cent), Mozambique (56 per cent), Mali (55 per cent), Burkina Faso and South Sudan (52 per cent), Malawi (50 per cent), Ethiopia (49 per cent), Sierra Leone...(48 per cent), Eritrea (47 per cent), Uganda (46 per cent), Somalia (45 per cent), Zambia (42 per cent), Congo, Madagascar and Senegal (39 per cent)....[T]he International Centre for Research on Women (ICRW)... added...Bangladesh to the countries with rates over 60 per cent, and...India, Nepal, Nicaragua and Tanzania to those with rates over 40 per cent. Unless figures in all these countries are brought rapidly down, gender-based

poverty and violence against girls will stand no chance of being eliminated." *5 Elaine Storkey

When UN Women, quoted above, states that child marriage "increases a girl's risk of experiencing domestic violence," that is quite an understatement. Most girls entering child marriage do so under strong coercion.

> "[C]hild, early and forced marriage is a confluence of the multiple violations of the rights of girls. It is about poverty, discrimination, and exclusion; it is violence against women and girls, abuse, rape and exploitation." *6 Nyaradzayi Gumbonzvanda

Girls entering coercive child marriages are "denied choice of marriage partner and/or sexual orientation" and experience "coerced sexual initiation, rape." *7 And that's just the beginning. For many girls, because of the coercion involved, child marriage becomes a lifelong form of institutionalized violence and abuse in the patriarchal family.

It is estimated that more than 200,000 child marriages occurred in the U.S. from 2000 to 2015. *8 In May 2020, Minnesota and Pennsylvania were on the verge of becoming the 3rd and 4th states in the U.S. to fully ban child marriages, joining Delaware and New Jersey.

> "Supporters point to research showing that teens in the U.S. who marry before 18 complete less education and face higher rates of poverty, mental health and drug problems later in life. They say underage girls are often coerced or forced into legal unions they cannot easily escape." *9 Torey Van Oot

Of course, child marriages help to reproduce Patriarchy as girls are subjugated to older men and serve to bolster the patriarchal family and patriarchal lineages.

> "Premature pregnancy and motherhood are an inevitable consequence of child marriage. An estimated 14 million adolescents between 15 and 19 give birth each year. Girls under 15 are five times more likely to die during pregnancy and childbirth than women in their twenties." *10

Child marriages block girls from developing into free and autonomous adults and instead result in great oppression of vulnerable girls.

Male dominance in the heterosexual patriarchal family often involves the use of force by husbands against wives. However, many men in the U.S. are also victims of domestic assault. Violence is not restricted to men. But when women are perpetrators of domestic violence it is sometimes in self-defense, the violence in general is usually not as severe as male violence, and the violence results in far fewer deaths. Overall, the large majority of perpetrators of domestic violence are men. Domestic violence is usually an effective means for a man to maintain dominance and enhance control over a subordinate female partner.

> "While each person is unique, personal experiences, individual characteristics, and social learning combine to produce in batterers a strong desire to control their intimate partners and a strong belief in the rightness of their domination. They attempt to establish and maintain this control by using a variety of oppressive tactics against their partners. In pursuit of domination, batterers learn that violence is a particularly effective strategy. Violence usually produces the immediate desired result—the decision is made, discussion is over, rebellion is crushed, control is maintained. The victim lives in fear of further violence, and alters her behavior to accommodate the abuser's moods, whims, and needs in order to protect herself. This oppressive system keeps the woman isolated and subordinate, making her escape difficult, if not impossible." *11 Minnesota Coalition For Battered Women

Among a variety of oppressive tactics, domestic violence is quite effective and is widely used by men all over the world.

As many have stated, the most dangerous place for a woman is in her home with her male intimate partner.

> "Most violence against women is perpetuated by current or former husbands or intimate partners. More than 640 million women aged 15 and older have been subjected to intimate partner violence (26 per cent of women aged 15 and older). Of those who have been in a relationship, almost one in four adolescent girls aged 15 to 19 (24 per cent) have experienced physical and/or sexual violence from an intimate partner or husband." *12 UN Women

Even before becoming a subordinate partner in a patriarchal family, many adolescent girls suffer assaults from males.

The patriarchal culture is very strong in all nations and means that all females may have legitimate fears of being assaulted. Domestic violence is often socially acceptable among men and institutionally supported.

"According to Michelle Bachelet, former UN Women Executive Director, up to seven in ten women continue to be targeted for physical and/or sexual violence in their lifetime. This is not helped by the fact that 603 million women live in countries where domestic violence is still not a crime." *13 Elaine Storkey

Since Michele Bachelet's November 2012 press release, more nations may have criminalized some forms of domestic assault. However, for most women, having laws on the books criminalizing domestic violence doesn't result in any real support. According to UN Women:

"Fewer than 40 per cent of the women who experience violence seek help of any sort....Fewer than 10 per cent of those seeking help appealed to the police." *14

Fewer than 4% (10% of 40% is 4%) of violently assaulted women seek police help—and understandably so. Patriarchal criminal legal systems are basically designed by powerful men and support male privileges—and so providing assistance to battered women usually does not happen.

"A 2014 E.U. Survey of 42,000 women across all 28 member states found that 26% of French women respondents said they [had] been abused by a partner since age 15, either physically or sexually....[I]t's 4 percentage points above the E.U. average and the sixth highest among E.U. countries....A [French] Justice Ministry report released this month [November 2019] acknowledged authorities' systematic failure to prevent domestic violence deaths....'When it comes to violence against women, it showed actually that police do very little to protect women who turn to them for protection'....The Justice Ministry report this month found that 41% of 'conjugal homicide' victims studied had previously reported incidents of domestic violence, and 80% of complaints sent to prosecutors went uninvestigated. 'Our system doesn't work to protect women,' Justice Minister Nicole Belloubet told French TV channel LCI." *15 Claire Parker

Patriarchy rules—all over the world—including France, Europe, and the U.S.A.

Domestic violence has always been commonplace in the U.S., which was created as a patriarchal, white-supremacist nation.

> "Every married man, no matter how poor, owned one slave—his wife....And every man, married or not, had a gender class consciousness of his right to domination over women, to brutal and absolute authority over the bodies of women....A man owned his wife and all that she produced....He also owned any personal property she might have....He also, of course, had the right to her labor as a domestic, and owned all that she made with her hands—food, clothing, textiles, etc. A man had the right of corporal punishment, or 'chastisement' as it was then called. Wives were whipped and beaten for disobedience, or on whim, with the full sanction of law and custom." *16 Andrea Dworkin

In the U.S., police forces and the legal system began as all-white-male institutions. The police and the criminal legal system not only did not offer any protection to wives from domestic violence—they viewed it as normal and incidental. So the U.S.'s patriarchal and racist legal system developed mainly to punish men for "real crimes" and not for domestic violence.

> "[C]onvicts punished by imprisonment in emergent penitentiary systems were primarily male. This reflected the deeply gender-biased structure of legal, political, and economic rights. Since women were largely denied public status as rights-bearing individuals, they could not be easily punished by the deprivation of such rights through imprisonment. This was especially true of married women, who had no standing before the law. According to English common law, marriage resulted in a state of 'civil death,' as symbolized by the wife's assumption of the husband's name. Consequently, she tended to be punished for revolting against her domestic duties rather than for failure in her meager public responsibilities....The persistence of domestic violence painfully attests to these historical modes of gendered punishment." *17 Angela Y. Davis

In the U.S., a long history of white supremacy, racism, Black slavery, and Native genocide has meant that women in America have experienced different amounts of privilege and oppression.

> "In a racially imperialist nation such as ours, it is the dominant race that reserves for itself the luxury of dismissing racial identity while the oppressed race is made daily aware of their racial identity." *18 bell hooks

Understanding various forms of oppression and their intersectionality is helpful for the cause of universal liberation. I believe that "the umbrella" of a very broad understanding of Patriarchy, combined with historical analysis, is a good basis for understanding various oppressions. Before there was racism, white supremacy, imperialism, and capitalism there was Patriarchy. In different nations Patriarchy undergoes changes, mutations, adaptations—and continues to thrive. Male dominance, female subordination, and patriarchal traditions cut across all classes, races, and ethnicities. And domestic violence continues at high rates among all classes, races, and ethnicities.

Not only has domestic violence persisted in the U.S. for centuries, it has continued on a massive scale.

> "In the USA, according to the US National Center for Injury Prevention and Control, women experience about 4.8 million intimate partner-related physical assaults and rapes every year, with, in 2007, an estimated 1,640 ending in death." *19 Elaine Storkey

The ancient, biblical, patriarchal curse on Eve: "yet your desire shall be for your husband and he shall rule over you" (Genesis 3:16) continues to be very strong in the U.S. and helps to maintain the patriarchal family. Patriarchal family traditions are carried forward by most weddings (and married life). Most heterosexual weddings are quite "traditional," that is, they are thoroughly patriarchal. The tradition of the father walking the bride down the aisle, symbolizing the giving of a daughter by the father to the male groom, is patriarchal. The traditional clothing and dress and appearance of the bride and groom and their entourage are patriarchal. A large number of women still follow the patriarchal tradition of changing their last name and accepting the surname of their husband. The traditional wedding and wedding reception usually involves the building and extension of the patriarchal family through the connecting of two families and lineages, adding new in-laws and relatives. The extended families and relatives are often a source of conflict and dysfunctional behavior. Yet, the patriarchal culture places a high value on maintaining the bonds and bloodlines of the extended patriarchal families.

When two people get married, especially two young adults, they usually do not have a deep understanding of Patriarchy. Everyone is immersed in patriarchal culture and society from their births. And everyone has internalized, in various amounts, patriarchal values. Therefore, when two people get married they are not only marrying their partner, they are also marrying into the patriarchal culture. The unconscious, unspoken pact is one of accepting as normative the mainstream patriarchal culture and lifestyle for their marriage. This is so even when one consciously deviates a little bit from the mainstream. But starting out a married life by marrying into the patriarchal culture gets a couple deeply entwined in the culture and makes later attempts to deviate from it more full of conflicts and troubles.

Due to evolution, biology, active hormones, and patriarchal culture, many *young* adults are driven to mate—and to reproduce the patriarchal family. And even though many people are supporting various progressive social justice issues to change society, many young adults are largely unaffected by these efforts and are mating, having children, and carrying forward patriarchal culture.

Like everyone else, people of color in the U.S. have strongly internalized patriarchal values. This patriarchal internalization needs to be an important part of analyzing and understanding the various forms of oppression they live under.

Black families have long been under attack in the white-supremacist U.S. Before the U.S. became a nation, Black families were torn asunder in Africa and shipped under atrocious conditions across the Atlantic Ocean to be sold into slavery in America. During the days of chattel slavery, Black families faced incredible adversity. White slaveholders often raped Black female slaves and violent beatings of all slaves were common. Black families were often torn apart by white slaveholders. After the end of chattel slavery, Black families continued under great stress from white racism and terrorism and various forms of economic and legal discrimination and exploitation. Black families have struggled greatly from housing discrimination, educational discrimination, job discrimination, bank-loans discrimination, police racial-profiling and brutality, the racist so-called "War on Drugs," racist environmental pollution, and racist mass incarceration.

Because of the powerful, historical forces working to break apart Black families, it should not come as a surprise that many Black families have either begun with absentee fathers or have broken down so that they consist only of a mother and her children. It would be inaccurate to simply describe families with a female head-of-household as "matriarchal" because this would obscure the reality that these families are still essentially patriarchal. (Since the whole world is patriarchal it is difficult to envision what Matriarchy would be like. Matriarchy could be defined as a community or society outside the domain of Patriarchy, completely independent from overarching male authority, and characterized by the prevailing leadership of women. I'm not aware of any examples.) The mothers in Black female-headed households usually have strong patriarchal values and beliefs, conform to feminine standards, and raise their children according to normative patriarchal masculine and feminine gender roles. The single mothers take on additional fatherly/masculine family duties besides their traditional motherly feminine duties—but this does not alter the traditional patriarchal family values that are supported.

In a complicated mix of Black-held patriarchal values and opposition to white racism a new organization was formed in Minnesota called Stop Child Protection Services From Legally Kidnapping (SCPSFLK).

"State data show that black children in Minnesota are slightly more than three times more likely than whites to be reported to child protection and to be removed from their homes. They [SCPSFLK] are pushing for stronger parental protections, including the right to use corporal punishment to discipline their children....'There is a lot of concern, particularly in the African-American community, that child protection doesn't understand their culture and is removing children that are doing OK,' said Rich Gehrman, executive director of Safe Passage for Children of Minnesota, a watchdog group for child welfare." *20 Chris Serres

Minnesota's white-dominated child-protection state-services have been disproportionately breaking up Black families. A Black-led group was organized to defend traditional patriarchal physical-force punishments of children, known as "corporal punishment." The culture that isn't fairly "understood" is the Black *patriarchal* culture that often uses corporal punishment of children. The point to be emphasized here is that, in general, people of color have patriarchal cultures and promote patriarchal family values regardless of whether or not their families have a male head-of-household.

Gays and lesbians in the U.S., who have long been oppressed in a heterosexist nation which has persecuted sexual minorities and viewed homosexuality as an inferior sexual orientation, often have strongly internalized patriarchal values. Same-sex relationships often mimic patriarchal heterosexual relationships with one person in a dominant role and the other in a subordinate role. Some lesbian relationships have a butch and a fem, patterning themselves in some ways similar to patriarchal gender roles of masculine and feminine. And similar to heterosexual relationships the dominant partner in same-sex relationships often resorts to domestic violence.

> "Partner violence toward lesbians is estimated to be between 22% and 48%....A lesbian batterer can use the bias in the criminal justice system to control her partner....The problem of violence in same sex relationships is widely ignored by both the straight and gay communities, and social institutions often refuse or fail to intervene to stop the lesbian or gay batterer." *21
> Minnesota Coalition For Battered Women

The point to be emphasized here is that even gay and lesbian relationships have internalized patriarchal values and do not represent much of an alternative to Patriarchy and the patriarchal family.

Homeless people in the U.S., who have long been stigmatized and oppressed in an exploitive capitalist economy which caters to the wealthy, usually have strongly internalized patriarchal values. Homeless people have often fallen away from their patriarchal families but hold on tightly to patriarchal values. Most homeless mothers with children raise their children according to traditional patriarchal gender roles of masculine and feminine. And social service agencies and organizations that help homeless people basically work to help homeless people be assimilated and re-integrated back into a patriarchal culture and society. Thus homeless people, who are at the bottom of society, in many ways continue to support a patriarchal society and do not represent any sort of groundswell against Patriarchy. Despite much advocacy for more social justice for homeless people,

Patriarchy continues to "win on the ground" through the lives of homeless people.

Jesus and the Discipleship/Liberation Movement

Humanity's only true hope for overcoming Patriarchy and saving the planet is through Jesus and his discipleship/liberation movement. Jesus' movement is the perfect antidote and alternative to the patriarchal family and all patriarchal institutions.

Jesus calls people to "come out" of Patriarchy and to be part of a new family that is based on commitment and discipleship to Jesus. The call is to break from loyalty to the patriarchal family and biological bloodlines and to prioritize commitment to Jesus and Jesus' new family. "Coming out" of Patriarchy means that Jesus' new family will be completely opposed to male dominance and female subordination that results in hierarchy, inequality, oppression, and violence. Instead, Jesus' new family is committed to Jesus' leadership, egalitarianism, equality, service, nonviolence, and love.

This doesn't make sense to many evangelical and fundamentalist Christians who adhere to a doctrine of supporting "family values." Family values to them can be translated as ironclad support for a patriarchal heterosexual nuclear family structure.

To break away from the patriarchal family and biological bloodlines will create divisions and great conflict. Jesus says,
"Do you think that I have come to bring peace to the earth? No, I tell you, but rather division! From now on five in one household will be divided, three against two and two against three; they will be divided: father against son and son against father, mother against daughter and daughter against mother, mother-in-law against her daughter-in-law and daughter-in-law against mother-in-law." (Luke 12:51-53)
The revolutionary Way of Jesus polarizes as people must choose which "pole" they are loyal to—either Patriarchy or Jesus. In this context of polarization and conflict Jesus says,
"Whoever is not against us is for us." (Mark 9:40)
Jesus' discipleship/liberation movement will draw out both support and opposition.

Jesus makes clear that his discipleship/liberation movement requires great commitment and the willingness to be part of a costly liberation struggle.

> "Now large crowds were traveling with him; and he turned and said to them, 'Whoever comes to me and does not hate father and mother, wife and children, brothers and sisters, yes, and even life itself, cannot be my disciple. Whoever does not carry the cross and follow me cannot be my disciple....So, therefore, none of you can become my disciple if you do not give up all your possessions." (Luke 14:25-27,33)

The commitment to Jesus and to be part of Jesus' new family of followers and disciples must be far stronger than the bonds that tie together the patriarchal family and biological bloodlines. Yes, Jesus teaches his followers to love all people, including beloved family members. But, in order to "come out" from Patriarchy and to form a new Jesus-centered family, Jesus' followers must connect most deeply with Jesus' family. This means detaching from their *patriarchal* family and letting their family members choose between the two poles (Jesus or Patriarchy). As Jesus mentioned above, this will bring divisions among family members. Also, Jesus' followers are to "carry the cross" of nonviolence and face the risk of deadly persecution. And they are to give up their wealth (if any) that they have gained in a patriarchal society if they are to become disciples and live within an egalitarian family/community.

While followers of Jesus who "come out" of Patriarchy detach from their biological families, possessions, and family inheritances, they also gain a new family, new possessions, and a new inheritance.

> "Peter began to say to him, 'Look, we have left everything and followed you.' Jesus said, 'Truly I tell you, there is no one who has left house or brothers or sisters or mother or father or children or fields, for my sake and for the sake of the good news, who will not receive a hundredfold now in this age—houses, brothers and sisters, mothers and children, and fields with persecutions—and in the age to come eternal life.'" (Mark 10:28-30)

Notably, as related in the above passage, Jesus' new family does not mention "fathers."

To break from Patriarchy and from the patriarchal family and lineages means making a definite and clear break from the dominative power and authority of "fathers." Jesus teaches,

> "And call no one your father on earth, for you have one Father—the one in heaven....The greatest among you will be your servant. All who exalt themselves will be humbled, and all who humble themselves will be exalted." (Matthew 23:9,11-12)

Jesus prohibits his followers from calling any man on Earth their "father." God becomes the substitute, or the real "Father," and the only "Father." In order to *tear the fabric of Patriarchy on the ground* God becomes the only "Father" to Jesus' new family. It is that important.

Jesus' new family must use the term "Father" exclusively for God. However, it is also essential for Jesus' followers not to use exclusively male God-language which reinforces all kinds of patriarchal ideologies, theologies, relationships, and institutions. Exclusively male God-language has made God into the image of men, as a male God who supports a so-called "natural order" of male dominance and female subordination. Therefore, it is essential to overcome patriarchal fragmentation and idolatry in God imagery by using female God-language and imagery for God. The creator God is both our true Father and Mother, creator of all. Female God-language and imagery is uplifting and healing and honors the wholeness of God and the essential goodness and equality of females. Christian use of female God-language is in its infancy and is needed to replace "the patriarchal mind" with "the mind of Christ."

The great liberation struggle to save humanity and to save the world is the struggle to overcome Patriarchy and to establish God's kingdom or commonwealth on Earth. It is a liberation struggle to overcome the global plague of patriarchal civilizations covering the surface of the Earth. By connecting closely with Jesus the liberation struggle develops deep roots. This is essential since the struggle to overcome Patriarchy must be won on the ground. The Messiah-led liberation struggle begins to sink strong roots when people come out of Patriarchy and become part of Jesus' new family.

Footnotes

1. Elaine Enns, Ched Myers, Healing Haunted Histories, A Settler Discipleship of Decolonization, Cascade Books, Eugene, Oregon, 2021, p. 227.
2. Fernando Belo, A Materialist Reading of the Gospel of Mark, Orbis Books, Maryknoll, New York, 1974, 1981, p.40.
3. UN Women, citing United Nations Department of Economic and Social Affairs, Statistics Division, 2020, website accessed 8-16-2021.
4. Emma Batha, Thomson Reuters Foundation, "'Covid generation' risks child marriage, forced labor, ex-leaders warn," Duluth News Tribune, August 19, 2020.
5. Elaine Storkey, SCARS ACROSS HUMANITY: Understanding and overcoming violence against women, IVP Academic, Downers Grove, Illinois, 2015, 2018, pp. 50-51.
6. Nyaradzayi Gumbonzvanda, of the World YWCA, quoted in SCARS ACROSS HUMANITY, p.53.
7. BWSS website.
8. SCARS ACROSS HUMANITY, citing Chris Baynes, The Independent, July 18, 2017, p. 51.
9. Torrey Van Oot, "Bill would raise minimum legal marriage age to 18," Star Tribune, May 7, 2020.
10. The State of the World's Children 2007, ?UNICEF.
11. Minnesota Coalition For Battered Women, "Understanding Battering," p. 5.
12. UN Women, citing World Health Organization, etc.
13. Elaine Storkey, p.80.
14. UN Women.
15. Claire Parker, AP, "French Women Demand Action," Star Tribune, November 24, 2019.
16. Andrea Dworkin, Our Blood: Prophecies and Discourses on Sexual Politics, Harper & Row, 1976, pp. 80,82.
17. Angela Y. Davis, Are Prisons Obsolete?, Seven Stories Press, New York, 2003, p. 45.
18. bell hooks, AIN'T I A WOMAN, p. 138.
19. Elaine Storkey, p. 79.
20. Chris Serres, "Effort to void child protection laws builds," Star Tribune, June 6, 2018.
21. Minnesota Coalition For Battered Women, "Understanding Battering," pp. 1,4,6.

Chapter 4

Patriarchy and Rape Culture

How hard is it to save humanity and to save the world? How hard is it to overcome Patriarchy? It is very, very hard—and "rape culture" highlights how hard it is.

For many people the term "rape culture" may seem to be hyperbole—an overstatement of the problem of rape. The term "rape culture" is fairly recent.
> "In the 1970s, feminists called the normalization of rape in popular culture 'rape culture,' referring to attitudes in advertising, movies, music, TV shows, and other media that dismiss or encourage sexual assault and rape." *1
> Nancy Jo Sales

For many people, though, use of the term "rape culture" may seem to be quite an exaggeration. However, in the big-picture context of Patriarchy, the term fits well. And I would expand its usage to be an apt description for patriarchal culture in general. Rape culture is an integral and inseparable part of a patriarchal society. Solving the problem of rape is not simply a matter of stopping, punishing, or changing a number of bad individuals. The problem of rape is much bigger than that. Rape culture is systemic. Rape culture is pervasive throughout a patriarchal society and "infects" people in different ways (through the inner workings of people's hearts and minds). Let us make a broad examination of rape culture.

<u>Roots and Characteristics of Rape Culture</u>

The roots of rape culture are the same as the roots of Patriarchy. The basic premise of Patriarchy is male dominance and female subordination, resulting in hierarchy, inequality, oppression, and violence. Patriarchy, through its various hierarchies, "fragments the whole." Patriarchy brings divisions between humans and God, between men and women, between white people and people of color, between humans and nature, and between mind and body. The resulting hierarchies and inequalities are very important. Hierarchies are based on inequality. Ultimately, without equality there is no justice.

People at the top of a hierarchy have some measure of dominative power over people lower in a hierarchy. Dominative power is "power over others." It is the power to rule over, govern, control, or dominate other people. *Dominative power is a morally-corrupting force.* As Lord Acton stated, "Power corrupts and absolute power corrupts absolutely." When women are integrated into patriarchal institutions and rise in an organizational hierarchy they also experience the same morally corrupting force as men. Thus, dominative power corrupts women too as they rise up in a hierarchy.

A patriarchal capitalist society with great economic inequalities strengthens male (in particular but also female) selfish materialistic desires. In a society with great economic inequalities, wealth is a form of power. *Wealth is also a morally-corrupting force.* Wealth leads to placing a high value on materialistic goods, pleasures, and an affluent lifestyle, and a lower value on the needs of other people. Wealth leads to a lessening of empathy for other people. Wealth and materialistic desires contribute to often viewing and treating people as objects.

Male dominance and power and the objectification of females often slides into male coercion and violence.

> "What are the roots of Violence Against Women?
> Violence against women is rooted in unequal power relationships between men and women in society. In a broader context, structural relationships of inequalities in politics, religion, media and discriminatory cultural norms perpetuate violence against girls and women.
> ....the forms of violence might be shaped differently based on factors such as sexual orientation, religion, ethnicity, class, age, nationality. Significantly, Immigrant and Aboriginal women are further marginalized due to ongoing racism.
> In a male-dominant society, male privilege becomes the norm and contributes to the belief and behaviour of men that they have the right to control women." *2 BWSS

Patriarchy gives rise to male dominance, male privilege, male entitlement, and widespread social approval for men to exert various amounts of control over girls and women. Much of that control can include coercion and violence.

Historically, male dominance and privilege go back as far as Patriarchy has existed. Male privilege has brought to men a consciousness of being far better off as a male rather than as a female.

> "It was a rhetorical commonplace that Hellenistic man was grateful to the gods because he was fortunate enough to be born a human being and not a beast, a Greek and not a barbarian, a free man and not a slave, a man and not woman. This cultural pattern seems to have been adopted by Judaism in the first or second centuries C.E. and found its way into the synagogue liturgy. Three times a Jewish man thanked God that he did not create him a gentile, a slave, or a woman....Consciousness of religious male privilege was widespread not only among Jews but among Greeks and Romans as well." *3 Elisabeth Schussler Fiorenza

Male privilege was and still is experienced by boys at an early age and by men all over the world.

Patriarchal hierarchies, male dominance, and male privilege contribute to male objectification of females. Male objectification of females has very serious and harmful consequences. Heterosexual men often view females as sexual objects—as objects for male viewing, judging, entertainment, control, and sexual pleasure. In turn, objectifying women as sex-objects leads to male fetishization of the female body. While women's breasts and genital area are greatly fetishized, all parts of the female body are subject to being judged by men according to patriarchal standards of beauty and desirability.

Patriarchal beauty standards for females are propagated through many institutions, traditions, education, parenting, social media, entertainment, and magazines. Females are enculturated to value their body according to the value placed on it by patriarchal beauty standards. Consequently, they feel pressure to try to conform to those standards. Through dieting, fashion, and cosmetics females attempt to reflect an ever-changing image of cultural beauty. The implicit devaluation of the natural body and appearance in patriarchal beauty standards works to alienate females from their bodies and results in a lot of self-shame and self-hatred.

Male objectification of females is often reflected through street harassment and many other forms of harassment of females.

> "In the Middle East and North Africa, 40-60 per cent of women have experienced street-based sexual harassment. In the multi-country study, women said the harassment was mainly sexual comments, stalking or following, or staring or ogling." *4 UN Women

Of course, street harassment of females by men is pervasive all over the world.

Male objectification of females is detrimental to both males and females. Objectification of another human being means a lessening of empathy for that person. One cannot view another person as an object and have much empathy for that person. Objectification of another person eases the path to harming that person. In military training and in war, male soldiers in particular are drilled and taught to objectify their enemies, often by referring to them with pejorative and racist slang. It is easier for soldiers to kill enemies who are viewed as objects or as sub-human. Likewise, male objectification of females is a form of dehumanization. It results in a loss of humanity (empathy) and moral integrity for males and increases the likelihood of violations of females.

Male dominance, male privilege, and male objectification of females is pervasive, although Patriarchy does have many variations. One obvious example of these things was a social media campaign in Afghanistan in 2017 that used a hashtag translated as #WhereIsMyName. In Afghanistan, some women were bravely trying to expand women's rights a little bit.

> "These are some of the terms Afghan men use to refer to their wives in public instead of their names, the sharing of which they see as a grave dishonor worthy of violence: Mother of Children, My Household, My Weak One or sometimes, in far corners, My Goat or My Chicken. Women also may be called Milk-sharer or Black-headed. The go-to word for Afghans to call a woman in public, no matter her status, is Aunt....Hassan Rizayee, an Afghan sociologist, said the custom was rooted in tribal ways of life. 'According to tribal logic, the important thing is the ownership of a woman's body,' Rizayee said. 'The body of a woman belongs to a man, and other people should

> not even use her body indirectly, such as looking at her. Based on this logic, the body, face and name of the woman belong to the man.' Reversing such deeply ingrained traditions will take a long time, he said." *5 Mujib Mashal

Afghanistan affords a look back at ancient Patriarchy and its traditions that are still strong today in some parts of the world.

Historically, women have been treated as male property, being given from fathers to husbands. As male property, rape in marriage was "institutionalized," i.e., the consent of the wife to sexual intercourse was unnecessary because she "belonged" to her husband. How much has changed over the millennia?

Marital and intimate partner rape continue to be widespread all over the world. Very large numbers of women are victims of marital and intimate partner rape—and virtually no men are prosecuted for marital rape and intimate partner rape.

> "Marital rape is not considered a crime in thirty-eight countries, including India, where the Research Institute of Compassionate Economics reports that the vast majority of rapists are the victims' own husbands." *6 Sohaila Abdulali

Incest-rape is also probably far more common than a society acknowledges—and also is very rarely punished.

Rapes of all types are vastly underreported. Only a small minority of rapes are reported to the authorities. Victims/survivors of rape often experience more shame and abuse from the male-dominant authorities after reporting a rape. Thus, the vast majority of men who commit the crime of rape go unpunished. The patriarchal, criminal legal system is extremely ineffective when handling reports of rape. This true all over the world. Take the U.K. for example.

> "Thousands of rape and sexual assault victims have been failed by the criminal justice system, according to a British government review released [June 2021] that cited a dramatic fall in convictions in England and Wales in recent years, prompting an apology from government ministers. In an interview with the BBC, Justice Secretary Robert Buckland said the findings revealed 'systemic failings,' to deal with complaints made by victims 'at all stages of the criminal justice process.'...The review was intended to address the decline in rape prosecutions, which the

> Ministry of Justice said fell 59%, and convictions, which have dropped 47%, since 2015-16. In that time, adult rapes jumped to 43,187 from 24,093, according to the Office for National Statistics. But the government estimates that fewer than 20% of rape cases are actually reported and that the number of victims is about 128,000 a year. Of reported cases, just 1.6% resulted in a person being charged....The review acknowledged that victims of rape have been treated 'poorly.'" *7 Aina J. Khan

Sexual assault and rape victims/survivors in the U.K. got a tardy government apology—which is cheap, often self-serving, and basically inconsequential.

Rape culture is an integral part of a patriarchal culture. Rape culture affects people in deep and often unacknowledged ways. Rape culture represents a type of societal terrorism against girls and women in particular. Rape culture represents a constant, but often dimmed, background of fear and terror for females.

> "In cultures with high levels of rape which go largely unpunished, I have often been told by women that the possibility of a violent attack is never far from their minds. It acts as a reminder of their powerlessness when confronted with brutal assault. Not surprisingly, across the world, women and girls limit their behaviour in a way that men and boys do not. Rape focuses the mind. Marshall University Women's Centre in West Virginia is right to suggest that 'rape functions as a powerful means by which the whole female population is held in a subordinate position to the whole male population, even though many men don't rape, and many women are never victims of rape.'" *8 Elaine Storkey

Rape culture, when viewed in a big-picture context, represents a form of societal terrorism and control over females which undergirds Patriarchy and goes mostly unacknowledged.

<u>Rape Culture in the United States</u>

Let us delve into the pervasive nature of rape culture in the U.S. Are patriarchal culture and rape culture one and the same?

Patriarchal culture in the U.S. has developed into a "hyper-sexualized" culture. Boys and girls in the U.S. are raised in this hyper-sexualized (rape) culture.

"A landmark 2007 report by the American Psychological Association (APA) found girls being sexualized—or treated as 'objects of sexual desire'...in virtually every form of media, including movies, television, music videos and lyrics, video games and the Internet, advertising, cartoons, clothing, and toys...The APA surveyed multiple studies which found links between the sexualization of girls and a wide range of mental health issues, including low self-esteem, anxiety, depression, eating disorders, cutting, even cognitive dysfunction. Apparently, thinking about being hot makes it hard to think: 'Chronic attention to physical appearance leaves fewer cognitive resources available for other mental and physical activities,' said the APA report." *9 Nancy Jo Sales

Girls are immersed in a "beauty-obsessed" patriarchal culture.
"Girls start out life now being immersed in princess culture, says Rebecca Hains, author of The Princess Problem: Guiding Our Girls Through the Princess-Obsessed Years....I think princess culture is part of the overall backlash against feminism....If you're hooked on external validation at age four, that plays into self-objectification and self-sexualization....'Beauty therapy' says the answer to problems like insecurity, peer pressure, etc. is always: look better, look beautiful, because that will raise your confidence and make you feel better about yourself. In 2015 there were more than 180,000 beauty gurus on You Tube, more than any other category." *10 Nancy Jo Sales

In a patriarchal culture boys and girls are raised differently—mostly according to patriarchal gender roles.
"[B]ehavior isn't born in an office petri dish. It's learned at a very young age. According to gender researcher Christia Brown, author of 'Parenting Beyond Pink and Blue,' research has shown there is little emotional difference between infant boys and girls. Both have the same capacity for sadness, both cry the same amount as babies and toddlers. What does change as kids reach preschool age is how those around them react to their crying or frustration. Tears suddenly become a sign of weakness, demarcated for girls, while boys are discouraged from showing vulnerability at all. Boys, however, are allowed to get mad—and get aggressive. 'Boys are taught very early on that aggression is

acceptable: Girls are given baby dolls and taught to be nurturing and compassionate, while boys are given action figures with guns in their hands,' Brown says. 'All toys are educational, and these toys educate children about what is acceptable behavior.'...'Even those little 3-year-old boys, we tell them, 'Man up,' 'Men in this family don't cry,' 'Suck it up,' 'Stop acting like a little girl' because we're not supposed to have those emotions, we're not supposed to be fearful, we're not supposed to be hurt and sad,' says Ted Bunch, the chief development officer at A Call to Men....How we express anger is a product of socialization, not DNA, says Bunch." *11 Jessica Machado

Social media is having some harmful effects and is strengthening the dysfunctional maturing of youth.
"Everybody is now using social media to self-promote, to craft an idealized online self, to present a sexualized self. The precipitous rise of narcissism in the American psyche —charted in studies since the 1970s—has been accelerated by social media....Social media causes so much drama it's anxiety-causing and depressing. It is distracting, time-consuming, and addictive....There has been an increase in anxiety and depression among teen girls that has been linked to sexualization and social media, and the ownership of smartphones....Studies have found that the winnowing away of face-to-face communication in the digital age may be having an effect on the ability of kids to interact in person....Kids...are not developing basic communication skills....When nonverbal cues are stripped away, it can limit the potential for understanding, arguably the foundation of empathy." *12 Nancy Jo Sales

Social media has become a platform for many abuses. The Internet has become a favorite medium for bullies, trolls, and predators. There is an increase in cyberbullying and harassment.
"Online harassment is pervasive but often hidden from view. According to Pew Research Center, 40 percent of Internet users have personally experienced harassment online, such as name-calling, sexual harassment and stalking. Young adults are the most likely demographic group to be victims, while women are often treated unfairly and harassed, the center said." *13 Sachi Jenkins

There is an increase in sexual cyber crime, particularly sextortion.

"One recent report, conducted by the FBI's internet Crime Complaint Center...found a 242% increase in cyber extortion crimes from 2017 to 2018....the report noted that the majority were 'part of a sextortion campaign in which victims received an e-mail threatening to send a pornographic video of them or other compromising information to family, friends, co-workers, or social network contacts if a ransom was not paid.'...71% of sextortion victims are under 18, according to the Brookings Institution....according to the Brookings report...91% of juveniles were manipulated through social media scams." *14 Andy Mannix

There is an increase in revenge porn.

"[V]ictims of nonconsensual pornography, which is sometimes called revenge porn [is] based on the notion that perpetrators often are jilted men sharing graphic images of their exes as a form of retaliation....The message boards and other platforms that are used to distribute revenge porn generally are protected from legal liability for user-posted content....Research indicates that victims of nonconsensual pornography experience similar trauma to sexual assault survivors....There continues to be a thriving marketplace for images obtained or disseminated against the will of the subject. 'The fact that this is what people want, that the kind of frisson that you get from this is that she didn't consent, that's about as close as you can get to an articulation of rape culture,' said Mary Anne Franks, president and legislative and tech policy director of the Cyber Civil Rights Initiative. 'That's literally saying: What you should be getting off on is the fact that she didn't say yes to this.'" *15 Jessica M. Goldstein

The Internet has made pornography easily accessible all of the time. Male domination of women, sexual objectification of women, sexual exploitation of women, and violence against women all come together in pornography. Pornography, of course, based on the above characteristics, strengthens rape culture.

"Our hypersexualized culture routinely objectifies women....Consider:
Fifty-four percent of American males admit to viewing porn frequently.

> Porn accounts for 25 percent of all internet searches—and 35 percent of all internet downloads....Not only is porn pervasive, it's stunningly misogynistic, demeaning and increasingly sadomasochistic.
> Eighty-nine percent of porn contains physical aggression. Women are the recipients of this violence 94 percent of the time.
> Pertinent to sexual harassment and assault, numerous studies demonstrate that exposure to porn markedly decreases viewers' empathy for victims. Other studies show that it increases men's dominating behaviors." *16 Mary Schiesel Middlecamp

The patriarchal pornography industry is a huge multibillion dollar industry with innumerable male customers. The pornography industry is an often unacknowledged spreader of the patriarchal ideology which buttresses and contributes to a rape culture. It spreads misogynistic stereotypes about and promotes abusive behaviors toward women and girls in particular. It objectifies, sexualizes, dehumanizes, and abuses women and children to fuel male fantasies, power trips, and sexual gratification. Pornography is primarily about male power to dominate women and children sexually and otherwise.

> "Confronting pornography and the powerful institutions which promote and protect it can be radicalizing for all women, especially perhaps for white women who, by virtue of living white in a racist society, may be tempted to imagine that privilege is the same thing as freedom, or that accepting tokenism will purchase truly human status. For pornography is relentless in its message, which is the message of the master to the slave: *This is what you are; this is what I can do to you*....all objectification is a prelude to and condition of slavery.... When we face the implications of the studies on pornography...we become aware that the glorification of violence against women is not a surface growth which can be deftly excised, leaving the anatomy around it untouched, it is systemic, and to question it is to question the entire society by which it thrives." *17 Adrienne Rich

As the Internet becomes regularly available to youth, pornography reaches a younger audience, contributing to the patriarchal maldevelopment of boys and girls.

"I mentor young men, and I see how the mainstreaming of pornography has hijacked their journey from adolescence to adulthood. Growing up is a difficult process, fraught with all sorts of emotional turmoil that tempt young men to look toward pornography for relief....In my experience, the consumption of pornography is nearly universal among young men, and the effects are never neutral....First exposure most often occurs during adolescence, when the brain is still forming and very impressionable by graphic images....Pornography is a sexual stimulant....it becomes a compulsive habit that retards maturation. It works a lot like drug use...But if the porn cycle is not broken...they grow up to be man-boys." *18 Johannes L. Jacobse

Like boys, girls that view a lot of pornography also develop a distorted perspective of sexuality.

"[Billie Eilish] began watching what she called 'abusive pornography' when she was 11. She eventually got to a point, she said, where she couldn't watch anything else. 'Unless it was violent, I didn't think it was attractive,' she said. 'I used to be like the person who would, like, talk about porn all the time. I would be like, 'Oh, it's so stupid that anyone thinks that porn is bad...I think it's cool and it's great.'...When she had her first sexual relationships, she said, she emulated what she had seen and ended up doing things she did not want to do. I doubt she is alone....

The proliferation of porn has warped how many young adults think about sex. Her habit came with a cost; porn was so upsetting to Eilish that she said she developed sleep paralysis, night terrors and nightmares. That doesn't surprise me. No one, especially a child, can unsee images of sexual degradation or violence. 'I feel incredibly devastated that I was exposed to so much porn,' she said. 'I think it really destroyed my brain.'" *19 Robin Abcarian

Not surprisingly, college campuses account for many rapes. While girls and women of all ages can become rape victims, the age group where women are most frequently raped is the age group from eighteen to twenty-four. Keith Edwards, "a speaker and consultant to higher education institutions on sexual violence," made a presentation at Minnesota's "first statewide summit on sexual violence on college campuses" in 2016.

"'Sexual violence is a men's issue. That's scary.'... Edwards said that studies have shown most men to be unaware of what actually constitutes sexual assault. Given a list of sex acts and asked to check which ones they have done themselves, 84 percent of respondents are unaware that an act they admitted to anonymously was illegal, Edwards said. 'They don't see the acts as rape, they are behaving normally,' Edwards said....When he talks to young men, Edwards talks about the posters of nude women on their dorm walls and the atmosphere of 'competitive recreational sex' at college." *20 Jon Tevlin

Many college fraternities are notorious for their role in a patriarchal rape culture.

"A study of sexual violence at Indiana University found that while only 12% of undergraduate men belong to fraternities, their houses are the sites of 23% of reported rapes....Sigma Alpha Epsilon (SAE) [is] one of the largest and wealthiest fraternities in this country....Undergraduate women at colleges across the country will tell you that SAE stands for 'Sexual Assault Expected.'...University administrators have shut down 30 SAE chapters and disciplined 130 others....Yet these same incubators of rape culture and general sadism are remembered with love by many of their former members." *21 Kevin O'Kelly

Fraternities help men form strong bonds with other men—but a lot of times these bonds are misogynistic. When it comes to sex, lots of young heterosexual men are focused on their own selfish sexual desires and sexual pleasure. They sexually objectify women, and have little or no concern about how sexual assaults affect women.

Many American girls get raped before they turn 18. "Over 3.3 million women's first sexual experience was rape, according to a new study of U.S. women ages 18 to 44, which also found that these incidents [sic] were associated with health problems later in life. The findings, published this week in the Journal of the American Medical Association, found that 6.5% of women in the U.S.—or about 1 in 16—experienced a sexual initiation that was forced or coerced. The average woman had this experience at age 15....'It's quite alarming, and that's just the tip of the iceberg because this study is only including women aged 18 to 44,' Laura Hawks, lead author of the study told NPR. 'You can imagine that if we asked this of women of all ages, the [absolute] number would be many millions higher.'" *22 Kayla Epstein

Many millions of American girls first sexual experience is that of getting raped. And where are the millions and millions of male rapists? Well, of course, they are everywhere—since rape occurs everywhere—and very, very few male rapists are held accountable and put in prison. (It would not be remotely possible to have enough prisons for all male rapists.)

Prostitution and Rape Culture

Male domination of women, sexual objectification of women, sexual exploitation of women, and violence against women all come together in the large-scale industries of sex-trafficking and pimping (i.e., prostitution).

Human trafficking is a significant contributor to various forms of modern-day slavery around the world. The different forms of slavery are all patriarchal. But the largest component of human trafficking is geared toward sexual exploitation of women and children.

> "Modern slavery involves 'millions of people who cannot walk away, who are trapped and denied freedom and lives of dignity, and bound only to serve and profit the criminals that control them.'...
>
> From their broad research, the International Labour Organization (ILO) estimated in 2012 that 20.9 million people globally are victims of forced labour, while the Global Slavery Index estimated that 48.5 million people were in some form of modern slavery in 167 countries.... People are trafficked for many purposes. Forced labour accounted for more than a third of trafficking from 2007 to 2010 and could be greater as detection rates vary....People are also trafficked for begging, illegal adoption, participating in armed combat, rituals and crime....The 2014 *Global Report* leaves us in little doubt that trafficking for sexual exploitation is still by far the biggest form detected worldwide." *23 Elaine Storkey

Storkey reports that 71% of global trafficking victims detected in 2014 were women and girls: "51 per cent were women, 20 per cent girls, 21 per cent men and 8 per cent boys."

Keeping in mind the big-picture context of a very broad understanding of Patriarchy, a very strong case can be made for the following two points: 1. Prostitution is mostly male sexual violence against women and children; and 2. Prostitution is essentially paid rape.

The pimping and prostitution industry basically institutionalizes male dominance and female subordination. The industry is fueled by male customers, by male demand for readily available sex-on-demand, i.e., for immediate sex through a quick and easy commercial transaction outside of any real relationship based on some degree of personal affection, personal regard, or equality. The supply of sex comes overwhelmingly from women and girls (although there is some male demand for sex with boys). Control of the industry is mostly male-dominated, although a significant minority of women have important positions in some regions of the world.

Prostitution is a dehumanizing trade based on the sexual objectification of women and children. Women and children, and girls in particular, become sexual objects and commodities to be bought and sold.
> "She is 'de-individualized and de-humanized,' bought and sold for all the distinctively female parts of her body." *24
> Elaine Storkey

Exploiting girls' and women's young adulthood in the sex industry to satisfy innumerable men's misogynistic sexual demands is so debasing of girls' and women's value, potential, and talents.

Women and children are often brought into the sex trade through a history of female powerlessness, coercion, deception, and mental and physical abuse. Very, very few college graduates are entering prostitution as their chosen profession. Instead, the people who are trafficked and prostituted are exploited based on a number of vulnerabilities. Some vulnerabilities are poverty, indebtedness, subordination of women and girls in patriarchal families and societies, traumatic child abuse, victims of historical militarism and colonization, racism, low education, unemployment, lack of a supportive social network, etc. These vulnerabilities provide an "underclass" of people to be exploited.

A great deal of coercion, grooming, abuse, and violence can go into making the "female product" ready for the male market.
> "In her authoritative article in *Psychiatric Times*, [clinical psychologist Melissa Farley] refers to prostitution as 'paid

> rape' and sees violence as the norm for women in prostitution. Incest, sexual harassment, verbal abuse, stalking, rape, battering and torture are all points on a continuum of violence which occur regularly. 'Prostituted women are unrecognized victims of intimate partner violence by pimps and customers...Pimps and customers use methods of coercion and control like those of other batterers: minimization and denial of physical violence, economic exploitation, social isolation, verbal abuse, threats and intimidation, physical violence, sexual assault, and captivity.'" *25 Elaine Storkey

Prostitution enables male misogyny as female prostitutes are repeatedly placed in very vulnerable positions to absorb the abuses of pimps and male customers.

Paying money for sex *does not cleanse* the prostitution business of all of the coercion, abuses, degradation of women and children, and violence that are inherently part of the business. Paying for sex also *does not absolve the male customers from responsibility* for all the abuses. On the contrary, the money and revenue from male customers is what drives the whole pimping and prostitution industry. Prostitution can be understood as a "more efficient" patriarchal form of rape. Prostitution provides men a patriarchally organized and "orderly" means of immediate access to women's bodies and genitals through economic power instead of through brute force. Yet, the "orderliness" of "paid rape" perpetuates never-ending human rights abuses against women and children.

> "So long as prostitution is seen merely as a myriad of individual acts of transactional sex, rather than a highly organized industry of paid rape, closely allied to trafficking, its harms are made invisible." *26 Elaine Storkey

The predominantly male buyers of sex basically come from mainstream society. A former prostitute, and survivor, from Dublin, Ireland commented on the ordinariness of male buyers of sex.

> "Do not for a moment think that the men paying to abuse here are not 'ordinary men.' I could not count the number of wedding rings and babies' car seats I encountered. The men who pay to debase and degrade women and girls in prostitution are the same men who play out the pretense of being happily married family men. I wonder

sometimes at the amount of women who would be shocked, not only to know their husbands are visiting prostitutes, but also to know the depth of their own husbands' contempt and misogynistic hatred of women." *27

Some nations, like the Netherlands in 2000, in order to regulate prostitution (and generate state tax revenues) legalized it. Efforts to legalize prostitution are based on a shallow analysis of prostitution and rape culture in patriarchal societies.

> "By legalizing prostitution, Dutch politicians opened up their cities to international organized crime, trafficking in women and children, and drug cartels. After only several years of the legalized results, Amsterdam mayor Job Cohen stated it was impossible to set up a safe zone for women in prostitution that was not controlled by organized crime. In 2008 the Dutch National Police Report confirmed that a clean, normal prostitution business sector in the Netherlands 'is an illusion.'…all the reasons given for how legalization would reduce trafficking, promote women's well-being in the sex industry, control child prostitution, and neutralize organized crime have not come true." *28 Janice Raymond

There is a lot of naïveté surrounding prostitution.

> "One survivor of prostitution…stated in response to the claim that prostitution was no better or worse than flipping burgers at McDonald's, 'In McDonald's, you're not the meat! In prostitution, you are the meat.'" *29

The demand for sex from men serving in the U.S. armed forces has often been recognized by commanding officers. In SE Asia a supply of women/prostitutes was deemed a priority and procured.

> "U.S. prostitution colonialism in the Philippines created the model for the U.S. military-prostitution complex in most parts of the world. Beginning in 1898 when the U.S. military took control of Manila from the Spanish forces that had occupied the Philippines since 1565, the United States established a system of prostitution that followed U.S. forces wherever they were based, particularly in Asia….in 1900….Journalist William B. Johnson reported American flags flew over the houses of prostitution in the red-light districts, the military licensed these brothels, and

> inspections were conducted under the supervision of the military government by what he called the 'department of prostitution.'" *30 Janice Raymond

The U.S. and Japan were enemies in World War II. After the war, the men in the U.S. armed forces and the men in the Japanese armed forces found common ground: the sexual exploitation of women and girls.

> "Historian Toshiyuki Tanaka has researched and written about Japan's violation of the 'comfort women,' estimated to affect over a hundred thousand mostly Asian women from Korea, the Philippines, and China who were victims of organized sexual slavery by the Japanese military during World War II. Japanese crimes against the 'comfort women' constitute for Tanaka 'a crime against humanity on an unprecedented scale.'...The fact that the 'comfort women' crimes were not prosecuted, he states, was owing to the 'sexual ideology' of the American occupation officials who were complicit in the establishment of a similar 'comfort' system for the U.S. military personnel in Japan." *31 Janice Raymond

Japan was never prosecuted or held accountable for its massive system of sexual slavery of women. And why not? Because the U.S. armed forces found common ground with the Japanese forces. And so this "crime against humanity," i.e., against women and girls, was not viewed by the American men in positions of authority as a crime to be prosecuted.

The U.S. military-prostitution complex has had long-term consequences.

> "During the 1990s, the wealth of the new Asian 'tiger economies' fueled an expansion of commercial sexual exploitation. New wealth created huge profits for sex industries and increased demand, with women from indigent rural areas recruited into the sex trade. Even poorer Asian countries such as Vietnam and Cambodia became destinations for sex tourists. Cambodia emerged as a leading country for child sex tourists seeking cheap sex with children; and Vietnam, flush with foreign investor cash, restored its sex industry to wartime highs....
> A 2005 University of Philippines study found that prostitution in the Philippines has become the fourth-largest source of gross national product (GNP) in the country. Developing countries like the Philippines have

become major centers for the global sex tourism industry. I witnessed this firsthand in 1998 on visits to Olongapo and Angeles City, where it was evident that former U.S. military bases, which had promoted a culture of prostitution in the local area, provided the infrastructure for a later sex tourism industry to thrive." *32 Janice Raymond

Were there any long-term consequences of the U.S. military-prostitution complex for the young U.S. servicemen returning to the U.S. from foreign military bases and/or foreign wars? The military-prostitution complex normalized "paid rape" — and obviously strengthened rape culture. Many servicemen became quite experienced with "paid rape," with viewing women and girls as sex objects, as commodities, and found pleasure in sexually exploiting them—and brought those experiences home with them.

Institutions and Rape Culture

Patriarchal institutions often harbor and protect a rape culture within them. It is part of a "natural tendency" for institutions to act in the interest of institutional self-preservation. With regard to rape culture this often means siding with the perpetrators of sexual harassment, assault, and rape. This manifests in trying to silence the victims while doing public relations work to preserve the good reputation of the institution.

The military's hierarchical command structure and gradations of rank is the epitome of patriarchal structure. It is the embodiment of dominative power and the antithesis of equality. So it is no surprise that rape culture and sexual assaults are part of the system. The patriarchal military has assimilated women into its forces, and many women are sexually assaulted. Republican U.S. Senator from Arizona, Martha McSally, who served 26 years in the Air Force, testified that:

> "she had been raped by a superior officer, one of multiple times she was sexually assaulted while she served her country….She said she did not immediately report the attacks….Later, when she began talking about them, she said she was so horrified about how her account was handled that she thought about quitting the Air Force. 'Like many victims, I felt like the system was raping me all over again,' McSally said….McSally's explanation of why

> she did not report the assaults is typical of both men and women in the military, who have historically feared retaliation from their peers or commanding officers. In 2014, the Pentagon released statistics based on a study conducted by the RAND Corp. that found that fewer than one-third of attacks in the military were reported, and that 52 percent of women who reported sexual assault said they had faced retaliation for doing so." *33 Emily Cochrane & Jennifer Steinhauer

In a rape culture the victims are often blamed and retaliated against while most perpetrators do not face any consequences.

Many men in the U.S. military have also been sexually assaulted, including multiple rapes. The perpetrators are preponderantly men.

> "On average, about 10,000 men are sexually assaulted in the American military each year, according to Pentagon statistics. Overwhelmingly, the victims are young and low-ranking....Women face a much higher rate of sexual assault in the military—about seven times that of men. But there are so many more men than women in the ranks that the total numbers of male and female victims in recent years have been roughly similar, according to Pentagon statistics—about 10,000 a year. And before women were fully integrated into the armed services, the bulk of the victims were men....A report published in May [2019] indicates that while the share of male victims who come forward has been rising recently, an estimated four out of five still do not report the attack. For tens of thousands of veterans who were assaulted in the past, the progress made in recent years offers little comfort. The damage has already been done. Many have seen their lives buckle under the weight of loathing and bitterness." *34 Dave Phillips

Men, like women, are also traumatized by being sexually assaulted and raped, and suffer long-term consequences.

Both girls and boys are vulnerable to sexual abuse in a rape culture. In the U.S., while most children who are sexually abused are girls, there are significantly large numbers of boys who are sexually abused.

> "1 in 20 boys is a survivor of childhood sexual abuse. The problem is often worse in group homes for troubled youth." *35 PVCA law firm

The PVCA law firm has worked with survivors from Watch Tower Bible and Tract Society of Pennsylvania (Jehovah's Witnesses), Kiwanis-sponsored group homes, the Catholic Church, the Church of Jesus Christ of Latter-day Saints, state-licensed foster homes, J-Bar Ranch, O.K. Boys Ranch, Toutle River Boys Ranch, and Echo Glen Children's Center. The point to be made here is that the sexual abuse of boys is very widespread, deep-rooted, and often institutionally situated in a patriarchal culture and society.

Of course, the very patriarchal Roman Catholic Church has been beset by child sexual abuse scandals for decades. The number of priests in the Roman Catholic Church's all-male priesthood who have sexually abused children is quite large. A recent grand jury investigation into just six Catholic dioceses in Pennsylvania issued a report naming over 300 Roman Catholic priests involved in abuses of children over a period of 70 years.

> "Avoid scandal. Use euphemisms. Ask inadequate questions. Lock complaints away in a 'secret archive.' Do not tell the police.
> Those are some of the tactics that leaders of the Roman Catholic Church in Pennsylvania used to conceal child sexual abuse by priests over 70 years, said a grand jury report….'It's like a playbook for concealing the truth,' said the grand jury….Special agents from the FBI's National Center for the Analysis of Violent Crime reviewed evidence collected by the grand jury, the report said, and identified a series of practices that were regularly used by the six dioceses to cover up reports of abuse. 'While each church district had its idiosyncrasies, the pattern was pretty much the same,' the report said. 'The main thing was not to help children, but to avoid 'scandal.'" *36 NY Times

The priests' sexual atrocities were compounded by the all-male Catholic hierarchy's deliberate efforts to protect the priests, cover-up their crimes, and leave the abused children to fend for themselves.

Another example of deeply-ingrained rape culture is the Boy Scouts of America. More than 82,000 men have come forward with claims of sexual abuse while in the Boy Scouts. The BSA filed for bankruptcy in February 2020.

> "The filing by the Boy Scouts of America for Chapter 11 bankruptcy protection is not about money. It's not about

> transparency or accountability or even making things right with adult survivors of child sexual abuse by BSA volunteers or staff. This bankruptcy is not about keeping kids safe. This bankruptcy is about secrecy and self-preservation....In 2019, a child sex abuse expert from the University of Virginia, Janet Warren, testified that she was contracted by the Boy Scouts of America to review all the Perversion Files the BSA had compiled from 1944 through 2016. Warren testified that her review of the files identified 7,819 perpetrators believed to have been involved in sexually abusing children....Each of these thousands of Perversion Files - again, their words—represents a moment in time when the Boy Scouts of America were faced with a moral choice: protect the children entrusted to their care or protect the reputation of the organization?...Over the years, the BSA has consciously chosen not to alert legal authorities to claims of sexual abuse against its volunteers and staff. It has chosen to handle these potentially scandalous situations 'in house,' keeping the information under its control. It is making the same choice with the Chapter 11 filing." *37 Jeff Anderson

Over many decades, BSA leaders continuously valued institutional self-preservation much more highly than reporting sexual abuse crimes against vulnerable boys. Information on abuses was relegated to secret files, protecting the child abusers and the organization.

The state's racist system of penal slavery is a system ideally suited for rampant sexual assaults and rapes. Jails and prisons are thoroughly patriarchal institutions based on dominative power, hierarchy, inequality, coercion, and violence. Prisoners are disproportionately people of color and poor people. Prisoners represent a class of people targeted by the state for punishments. But the punishments were not supposed to include being victimized by sexual assaults and rapes. Both men and women prisoners are preyed upon, but around 90% of prisoners are men.

> "Approximately one in five male inmates in the United States has faced forced or pressured sexual contact in custody, according to studies on the subject by researchers such as Cindy Struckman-Johnson at the University of South Dakota. One in 10 has been raped. For women, whose abusers are often corrections officers,

the rates of sexual assault are as high as one in four in some facilities....We need to recognize that none of the more than 2 million people now held in U.S. jails and prisons was sentenced to be raped." *38 Lara Stemple, Wendy Patten, Benjamin Jealous

The state's racist system of penal slavery does not reduce sex crimes. It is part of the rape culture and functions to propagate sex offenders—from the ranks of both the prison staff and the prisoners.

The very important topic of mass rapes as a deliberate weapon of war will be deferred to chapter 7.

This little overview of Patriarchy and rape culture is not intended to be thorough and complete. It is intended to highlight some key components of rape culture and to show that rape culture is an integral part of Patriarchy. Patriarchal culture can be described as rape culture—and it can be surmised that patriarchal culture cannot exist without rape culture.

<u>Jesus and the Discipleship/Liberation Movement</u>

Bringing rape culture to an end means bringing Patriarchy to an end. There is only one way to accomplish that: through Jesus and the discipleship/liberation movement.

Jesus calls people to "come out" of Patriarchy and to follow him. Part of "coming out" of Patriarchy means having a "change of mind" by uprooting the "patriarchal mind" and putting on "the mind of Christ." A patriarchal mindset views women and children as subordinate to men and often leads men to sexually objectify women and children. Add machismo, aggressiveness, coercion, and violence to this objectification and a rape culture ensues. The patriarchal mindset runs deep within men, in particular, and affects how they see other people. Jesus teaches:

> "You have heard that it was said, 'You shall not commit adultery.' But I say to you that everyone who looks at a woman with lust has already committed adultery with her in his heart. If your right eye causes you to sin, tear it out and throw it away; it is better for you to lose one of your members than for your whole body to be thrown into hell." (Matthew 5:27-29)

The above strong statement by Jesus is appropriate to counter a pervasive and lecherous patriarchal rape culture. How people

"see" with their eyes and their minds is so important. To see people as sexual objects is dehumanizing and leads to a loss of empathy and to a myriad of abuses. Jesus teaches:
> "The eye is the lamp of the body. So, if your eye is healthy, your whole body will be full of light; but if your eye is unhealthy, your whole body will be full of darkness. If then the light in you is darkness, how great is the darkness!" (Matthew 6:22-23)

A patriarchal mindset keeps men, in particular, in moral, ethical, and spiritual darkness.

Another part of "coming out" of Patriarchy means "deconstructing" some of the foundations of patriarchal culture, which includes rape culture. It means relinquishing dominative power, wealth, and privileges—which are morally corrupting forces.
> "As he was setting out on a journey, a man ran up and knelt before him, and asked him, 'Good Teacher, what must I do to inherit eternal life?' Jesus said to him, 'Why do you call me good? No one is good but God alone. You know the commandments: 'You shall not murder; You shall not commit adultery; You shall not steal; You shall not bear false witness; You shall not defraud; Honor your father and mother.' ' He said to him, 'Teacher, I have kept all these since my youth.' Jesus, looking at him, loved him and said, 'You lack one thing; go, sell what you own, and give [the money] to the poor, and you will have treasure in heaven; then come, follow me.' When he heard this, he was shocked and went away grieving, for he had many possessions." (Mark 10:17-22)

The rich man was well-established within patriarchal society. The unusual addition to the commandments of "you shall not defraud" seems to imply that this rich man, or rich men in general, generated wealth through exploiting their laborers. Regardless, Jesus' answer points toward reversing the direction of this flow of wealth from poor laborers to the rich. Jesus says, "you *lack* one thing." Ironically and revolutionarily, what the rich man *lacks* is his holding of wealth—which symbolizes his *lack* of love and empathy for the poor who lack basic necessities. Jesus' answer is for a redistribution of wealth, with the rich man giving all to the poor, and then for the man, freed from his possessions, to follow Jesus. The rich man's wealth was *prima facie evidence* of his failure to love his neighbors as himself. Holding on to wealth lessened the man's empathy and compassion for the poor. It supported patriarchal divisions, class divisions, between people. In order to follow Jesus, to develop more empathy, and to love one's neighbors as oneself, relinquishment of wealth is necessary.

Jesus calls people to "come out" of Patriarchy and to join a discipleship of equals with no relationships of domination and subordination.

"'Whoever does not receive the *basileia* [kingdom/ commonwealth] of God like a child (slave) shall not enter it.' (Mark 10:15) This saying is not an invitation to childlike innocence and naïveté but a challenge to relinquish all claims of power and domination over others....Thus liberation from patriarchal structures is not only explicitly articulated by Jesus but is in fact at the heart of the proclamation of the basileia of God." *39 Elisabeth Schussler Fiorenza

Jesus' discipleship of equals is intended to be nonhierarchical and egalitarian.

"Jesus called them and said to them, 'You know that among the Gentiles those whom they recognize as their rulers lord it over them, and their great ones are tyrants over them. But it is not so among you; but whoever wishes to become great among you must be your servant, and whoever wishes to be first among you must be slave of all.'" (Mark 10:42-44)

In Jesus' discipleship of equals there are to be no leadership positions and titles, and no one with dominative power and authority over others. Jesus teaches,

"The greatest among you will be your servant. All who exalt themselves will be humbled, and all who humble themselves will be exalted." (Matthew 23:11-12)

The spread of Jesus' worldwide movement means reducing the prevalence of social hierarchies.

Patriarchal dominative power is to be replaced with discipleship, humility, and service. Humility is lowly, staying connected to the ground, selfless, serving the common good, and positioning oneself to be a clear channel for God's love and Spirit-power. Thus, "coming out" of Patriarchy means relinquishing dominative power, wealth, and privileges—and through following Jesus becoming a "new creation" committed to overcoming Patriarchy and working for a New Creation over all the Earth.

Footnotes

1. Nancy Jo Sales, <u>American Girls: Social Media and the Secret Lives of Teenagers</u>, Alfred A. Knopf (Penguin Random House), New York, 2016.
2. BWSS (Battered Women's Support Services).
3. Elisabeth Schussler Fiorenza, <u>In Memory of Her: A Feminist Theological Reconstruction of Christian Origins</u>, Crossroad, New York, 1983, p. 217.
4. UN Women, based on a 2017 study.
5. Mujib Mashal, NY Times, "Afghan women ask: 'Where is my name?'," <u>Star Tribune</u>, July 31, 2017.
6. Sohaila Abdulali, <u>What We Talk About When We Talk About Rape</u>, The New Press, New York, 2018, pp. 120-121.
7. Aina J. Khan, NY Times, "U.K. apologizes to rape victims for a failed justice system," <u>Star Tribune</u>, June 20, 2021.
8. Elaine Storkey, <u>SCARS ACROSS HUMANITY: Understanding and overcoming violence against women</u>, IVP Academic, 2015, 2018, p. 125.
9. Nancy Jo Sales, pp.13-14.
10. Nancy Jo Sales.
11. Jessica Machado, Washington Post, "Help boys feel emotion to avoid raising angry men," <u>Duluth News Tribune</u>, June 5, 2018.
12. Nancy Jo Sales.
13. Sachi Jenkins, Reuters, "Tech panel: Online harassment, sexism must be met head-on," <u>Duluth News Tribune</u>, March 13, 2016.
14. Andy Mannix, "Kids face the silent terror of sextortion," <u>Star Tribune</u>, October 27, 2019.
15. Jessica M. Goldstein, Washington Post, "Pandemic is fueling boom in revenge porn," <u>Star Tribune</u>, November 29, 2020.
16. Mary Schiesel Middlecamp, "Look no further than a culture permeated with porn," <u>Star Tribune</u>, November 22, 2017.
17. Adrienne Rich, Afterword, <u>Take Back the Night: Women on Pornography</u>, Laura Lederer, editor, William Morrow and Company, Inc., New York, 1980, pp. 314, 320, 316.
18. Johannes L. Jacobse, "Affliction," <u>Star Tribune</u>, February 12, 2017.
19. Robin Abcarian, Los Angeles Times, "Tell your kids that Billie Eilish says porn destroyed her brain," <u>Star Tribune</u>, December 27, 2021.

20. Jon Tevlin, "Why campus rape is a men's issue," <u>Star Tribune</u>, June 12, 2016.
21. Kevin O"Kelly, "'True Gentlemen' [by John Hechinger] analyzes the troubling co-dependence of colleges and fraternities," <u>Duluth Reader</u>, October 5, 2017.
22. Kayla Epstein, Washington Post, "Millions say first sexual experience was rape," <u>Star Tribune</u>, September 22, 2019.
23. Elaine Storkey, pp. 100,101,106.
24. Elaine Storkey, p. 117.
25. Elaine Storkey, p. 115.
26. Elaine Storkey, p. 117.
27. Quoted in <u>NOT A CHOICE, NOT A JOB: Exposing the Myths About Prostitution and the Global Sex Trade</u>, p. 44, by Janice G. Raymond, Potomac Books, Washington, D.C., 2013, citing "The Harsh Realities of Being Raped for a Living," <u>Irish Examiner</u>, February 17, 2012.
28. Janice G. Raymond, <u>NOT A CHOICE, NOT A JOB</u>, Preface, p. xv.
29. Janice G. Raymond, p. 28.
30. Janice G. Raymond, pp. 152-153.
31. Janice G. Raymond, p. 157.
32. Janice G. Raymond, pp. 131,133.
33. Emily Cochrane & Jennifer Steinhauer, NY Times, "'Powerless': Air Force pioneer McSally says she was raped by superior officer," <u>Star Tribune</u>, March 8, 2019.
34. Dave Phillips, "Men Tell Their Stories of Rape in the Service," <u>New York Times</u>, September 12, 2019.
35. PVCA law firm, www.PVCA.law, <u>Prison Legal News</u>, July, 2021.
36. NY Times, "It's like a playbook for concealing the truth," <u>Star Tribune</u>, August, 2018.
37. Jeff Anderson, "Bankruptcy conceals hidden perils," <u>Star Tribune</u>, February 23, 2020.
38. Lara Stemple, Wendy Patten, Benjamin Jealous, "Doing something about prison rape," published in signonsandiego.com, September 26, 2003.
39. Elisabeth Schussler Fiorenza, pp. 148,151.

Chapter 5

Intersections Between Patriarchy, Gender, and Transgender

The big-picture context for every issue, problem, or topic is a very broad understanding of Patriarchy and how Patriarchy is bringing the world to ruin. Basically, Patriarchy represents a "social totality," affecting everything and within which everyone is born, raised, and lives.

The topic to be examined closely here is intersections between Patriarchy, gender, and transgender. Putting the analysis into its proper context in a patriarchal society is crucial. A special focus will be on the transgender pathway in the U.S. as it relates to children and youth under the age of 18. While the focus is more on children, adults are still involved in every step along the way. Transgender adults, age 18 or older, are generally not a concern of this chapter except for their partaking in various transgender affirming medical surgeries.

Properly examining intersections between Patriarchy, gender, and transgender is complicated and problematic. The topic is polarizing—as it must be—since the analysis critiques strongly held believes about gender. It provokes strong emotions and runs into high levels of ideological intractability. But a critique that recognizes the big-picture context of Patriarchy is warranted since both the political left and the political right can offer misguided paths forward—stemming from their rootedness in Patriarchy.

The political left is very intolerant of criticism toward any group that is part of their LGBTQ+ acronym. It is not "politically correct" to criticize any part of this grouping to such a degree that questioning and critiquing any part is sort of "taboo." Anyone who critiques the transgender pathway for children may be mislabeled as transphobic and vilified by the political left. The word "transphobic" is bandied about so much against anyone who does not *fully support* the pro-trans agenda that the word has really lost much of its true meaning in general usage. The political left supports the liberal reformist push, with its short-term goals and benefits, for "fully" integrating transgender groups into the larger heterosexist patriarchal society. It supports the integration of transgender groups into the patriarchal legal system and other major patriarchal institutions—but without changing the basic foundations of Patriarchy.

Before addressing the intolerance of the political right let us bring in the topic of "heterosexism."

Of course, Patriarchy, based on male dominance and female subordination, in varying degrees, supports sexism which includes stereotypical sex roles and sex-based discrimination against and oppression of females. Also, since a solid majority of people are heterosexual, and since the patriarchal family, often with a heterosexual male head-of-household, is a bedrock for supporting and reproducing Patriarchy, heterosexism predominates. Heterosexism is based on a heterosexual norm and a heterosexual orthodoxy—and it supports prejudices, discrimination, and oppression against women and sexual minorities.

The strength of Patriarchy, sexism, and heterosexism varies, with ebbs and flows, among nations. Waves of women's and gay rights' reform movements in the U.S. have reduced the strength of, but not overcome, heterosexism in the U.S. In particular, progress towards social acceptance and affirmation of homosexuality has grown significantly, which is very good. Homosexuality has become somewhat normalized in much of mainstream society and homosexual rights have been written into many laws. Even so, the enduring heterosexist patriarchal culture makes it much more difficult for young children and youth who are homosexual/queer to experience peer-group equality and strong parental support. Adverse reactions from peers and parents to their homosexuality places a heavy emotional burden on many gay and lesbian youth, and negatively affects their mental health.

The push for social justice for gays and lesbians has expanded to other sexual minorities that feel the heat and oppressive power of heterosexism. An acronym that lumps various sexual minorities together and is commonly used is LGBTQ+. An even longer acronym is LGBTTT-SIQQAA—which refers to lesbian, gay, bisexual, transgender, transsexual, Two-Spirit, intersex, queer, questioning, asexual, and agender. *1 Sexual minorities in the U.S. can experience a lot of discrimination, emotional stress, harassment, bullying, and "hate crimes," including violent assaults and murders. Transgender people can face much rejection and hostility.

> In 2020, the Human Rights Campaign documented at least 44 killings of transgender and gender-nonconforming people in the United States....Most of the victims were Black or Latinx trans women....Trans women of color experience discrimination at the intersections of racism, sexism, transphobia and homophobia, according to the campaign—meaning they are often denied safety, housing, jobs, healthcare and other basic rights." *2 Madeleine Davison

In this context of Patriarchy and heterosexism the political right has developed increasingly high levels of intolerance for perceived threats to their traditional patriarchal and white-supremacist worldview. The political right is pushing hard on issues relating to race (e.g., book banning, opposition to "critical race theory," voter suppression, stifling immigration, opposition to Black Lives Matter) and gender. Stemming from deep roots in sexism and heterosexism the political right has put a great deal of emphasis on topics like abortion and homosexuality. Recently, another topic has been added which represents another deviation from heterosexual orthodoxy—namely, transgender rights. The political right is pushing lots of legislation in many states concerning transgender issues, and often including the whole LGBTQ+ grouping. The legislative strategy enlists coercive and oppressive state power to reinforce heterosexism. Much legislation criminalizes medical interventions for transgender youth, threatens punishments for medical professionals or parents, increases various school regulations and restrictions, and, in general, contributes to a hostile environment for transgender youth. A rise in the level of social hostility towards LGBTQ+ people encourages more homophobia, transphobia, social aggression, and oppression. Also, some people on the political right continue to support so-called "conversion therapy," which may be defined as:

> "any practice or treatment that seeks to change an individual's sexual orientation or gender identity, including efforts to change behaviors or gender expressions." *3

Some unfortunate youth are sent to conversion/indoctrination sessions against their will and the coercive and oppressive experience can be traumatic, harming their mental health. Since the political right is currently pushing hard on transgender (and LGBTQ+) topics, any critique of the transgender pathway for children must bear in mind the current context and clearly differentiate itself from the political right.

There are many people today who are questioning gender, sex roles, and social norms and expectations. Many are seeking to affirm "alternative" identities. This individual search for personal identity and for how to fit into society and/or change society isn't necessarily very helpful for overcoming Patriarchy. The following analysis shows how Patriarchy is interwoven into mainstream gender roles and into many of the decisions of adults and children who firmly support the transgender pathway for children.

The term "transgender," in general, refers to people who have experienced what is sometimes called "gender dysphoria" — a profound dissatisfaction with one's body, sex, and gender category. Transgender people generally "move away" from their original sex, with many identifying themselves with the opposite sex. However, the term "transgender" has broadened in meaning, allowing a larger and more diverse group of people to identify as transgender.

> "I debunk a common misconception that all trans people are on what I call a 'binary' pathway, or moving from one side of the M-to-F [Male-to-Female] binary to the other, and I will introduce three sometimes-overlapping groups of people under the 'T': transgender people who are women or men, nonbinary transgender people who are neither, and people who are gender-fluid." *4 Lee Airton

Gender identity choices are increasing. And the number of people who identify as transgender is increasing—although accurate statistics are hard to come by. In 2011 the Williams Institute at the UCLA School of Law calculated that about 0.3% of the adult population in the U.S., about 700,000, identified as transgender. In 2016 it calculated that 0.6% of the adult population, around 1.4 million identified as transgender. And many children are identifying as transgender, significantly increasing the number of transgender people. Also not all transgender people have "come out" as transgender. Some are "closeted" and undercover. Thus, the numerical trend is toward an increasing number which can only be roughly estimated.

In order to examine the "transgender pathway" it is very important to differentiate in some ways "sex" from "gender." "Gender" is closely related to "sex" but they are not the same. "Sex" is based on biology, anatomy, chromosomes, hormone prevalence, and the reproductive system. The vast majority of people fall into two categories of "sex"—either "male" or "female." Only a very small number of people have some anatomical, chromosomal, hormonal, or reproductive abnormalities and may be termed "intersex."

> "Intersex is an umbrella term encompassing various conditions in which internal sex organs and external genitalia develop differently than for a typical boy or girl. Experts say roughly one in every 2,000 newborns has so-called differences of sex development." *5 David Crary

"Gender" is closely correlated with "sex" but is more expansive than biological sex. "Gender" may involve either *individualistic or societal "interpretations"* of "male" and "female." "Gender" may refer to an "inner sense" of "male" or "female" identity (or variations thereof) which are *individualistic* interpretations. Or, "gender" may refer to socially-accepted gender roles which are *societal interpretations* of "male" and "female."

The transgender-affirmative culture prioritizes *individualistic interpretations* of "male" and "female," resulting in each individual declaring their "true gender identity." Accordingly, one's "true gender identity" is then supposed to reveal one's "true sex."

> "Gender identity, as the ACLU defined it, is a 'medical term for a person's 'deeply felt, inherent sense' of belonging to a particular sex.'" *6

When one's "true gender identity" is an *individualistic interpretation* it is very subjective and does not need to correspond to any biological or physical evidence. In fact, for transgender people on the "binary pathway," their initial declaration of their "true gender identity" runs counter to the physical evidence, thus resulting in "gender dysphoria" (or "gender incongruence"). Someone who has been physically identified as "male" may decide that they are really a transgender female. Or, someone who has been physically identified as "female" may decide that they are really a transgender male.

When one's "true gender identity" is definitively decided by each individual in their mind it is possible for one's gender identity to be changeable whenever an individual decides to change it. So, a transgender person may be "gender-fluid." For example, a gender-fluid person may for a period of time decide that they are "male," and then decide for a period of time that they are "female."

Also, allowing for more internal self-discovery and questioning, an individual may settle on a gender identity of "non-binary." A "non-binary" individual may decide they are neither "male" nor "female." They cannot accurately describe themselves as either "male" or "female." They are "non-binary."

The transgender-affirmative culture is founded on the legitimacy and "truth" of *individualistic interpretations* of "male" and "female." Each individual's self-determined gender identity then clarifies for most trans people (but not for all) one's "true sex." The transgender-affirmative culture finds it to be offensive and insensitive whenever anyone questions a transgender person's self-declared gender identity. Since gender identity is decided by each individual alone, it is not supposed to be subjected to anyone else's questioning.

While the transgender-affirmative culture prioritizes *individualistic interpretations* of "male" and "female," *societal interpretations* of "male" and "female" still play a very large role. Many transgender people are on the binary pathway of moving from male to female or from female to male. Many, but certainly not all, transgender people have an underlying acceptance of *societal interpretations* of "male" and "female": the masculine gender role for males and the feminine gender role for females. Many transgender people move to the opposite sex and adopt society's gender role for that sex.

> "There is absolutely nothing wrong with being a woman who strongly identifies as a woman and loves all things associated with feminity, or being a man who strongly identifies as a man and loves all things associated with masculinity. Many transgender people feel this way, and many cisgender people feel this way too." *7 Lee Airton

Many transgender people who are on the binary pathway make a social transition to the opposite sex, adopt society's gender role for the opposite sex, and seek to fit in and "pass" socially as "normal" members of the opposite sex.

Is there "absolutely nothing wrong" with supporting *societal interpretations* of "male" and "female"? The terms "masculine" and "feminine" refer to patriarchal gender roles for males and females. Patriarchal gender roles are patriarchal social constructs—basically stereotypes. They provide behavioral expectations, guide development, and put social pressure on males and females to conform to them. Masculine and feminine gender roles are foundational for the maintenance of a patriarchal society. Although in different nations patriarchal gender roles will have variations, they all have the purpose of reinforcing a patriarchal, heterosexist society based in various degrees on male dominance and female subordination. So the patriarchal gender roles of "masculine" and "feminine" inherently support sexual inequality, patriarchal hierarchies, and patriarchal institutions. They inherently have an oppressive component to them which overrides any virtues they prescribe. For transgender children to accept patriarchal gender roles and to seek to conform to either gender role serves to strengthen and to reproduce Patriarchy.

The transgender-affirmative culture has adopted terminology to support transgender transitioning. The trans-culture uses the phrase "sex assigned at birth" to indicate the sex that a new-born baby was identified with on their birth certificate. The phrase indicates that this sex was not chosen by the baby. Rather, it was designated externally by people who could not know for certain what a baby's "true gender identity," and thereby "true sex," really is. As such, the so-called "sex assigned at birth" cannot be regarded as permanent and instead reflects just a particular moment in time. More important, according to the trans-affirmative culture, is for each individual to decide their own gender identity and sex. The terminology "sex assigned at birth" serves to de-legitimize and de-emphasize one's birth sex and to legitimize transitioning to the other sex (or to another gender-category). This terminology represents a detachment (and alienation) from one's physical body (as is represented by "gender dysphoria"). It attempts to normalize that detachment in order to ease the path to even greater detachment from one's "original sex." So, is there anything questionable about that?

What are some characteristics of Patriarchy that are relevant here? In general, Patriarchy "fragments the whole," breaks it down into separate parts, and exploits the parts. Pertinent here is how Patriarchy "fragments" a human being, bringing about the patriarchal mind-body dichotomy. The mind is dominant, rationalizes some degree of alienation and separation from the body, and subjects the body to repression, manipulation, and exploitation. The patriarchal mind-body dichotomy is strongly operative in the mainstream patriarchal gender roles of "masculine" and "feminine."

The transgender-affirmative culture can be seen as also strongly supporting the patriarchal mind-body dichotomy. In general, in most transgender people, and especially in transgender children, the mind and body are at odds with each other. The physical reality of the body, and especially, but not only, the genitals, does not match up with what one's mind determines is one's true gender and true sex. In any case, the mind is at odds with its physical body, determines the "reality" it wants (i.e., one's true gender identity and true sex), and determines in what ways one's body is to be subjected to manipulation and change by the patriarchal medical-pharmaceutical industry. (More will be said about the patriarchal mind-body dichotomy later in this chapter.)

The binary transgender pathway usually involves one or more of the following four steps: 1. Social transitioning; 2. Puberty blockers; 3. Cross-sex hormone treatments; and 4. Various surgeries (usually restricted to adults). The first step, social transitioning, involves repositioning oneself, with regards to sex and stereotypical gender roles. Steps 2-4 involve medical interventions.

Children who are interested in the transgender option may be encouraged by supportive adults to get on the transgender pathway at a very young age.
> "Trans activists argue that children should start social transition in kindergarten, puberty blockers at nine, cross-sex hormones at sixteen, and surgery at eighteen." *8
> Ryan T. Anderson

Of course the actual timeline for children on the transgender pathway varies a lot and many transgender children do not take all four steps. But the above timeline shows that many children, who are at a young age and a vulnerable stage in their physical and mental development, are encouraged by adults to make very serious changes in their lives.

Many children are learning about the transgender option at a very young age. In today's digital society, with easy access to the internet, no age is too young for a child to identify as transgender. Some parents want to give their young children more freedom to choose their gender and their "true sex."
"A very small but growing group of parents is using GNPs [gender-neutral pronouns] for their babies and toddlers (usually singular *they*) until these kids can make their gender and pronoun wishes known of their own volition." *9 Lee Airton

Why not let babies and toddlers figure things out on their own? Is it possible that some very young children are being offered "pseudo-freedom" and "pseudo-choices" concerning choosing their "true gender identity"? How much freedom should children be given?

There has been growth in the number of jobs for pro-trans adult counselors in schools and in Gender Identity Clinics. The pro-trans adult counselors are very supportive of young children taking step 1 in the transgender pathway of starting to make a "social transition." The "social transition" moves children into the standard societal gender role of the opposite sex in terms of clothing, behavior, bathrooms, different first names, different pronouns, etc. Children at a very young age start rehearsing and practicing the patriarchal gender role of the opposite sex in a deliberate way and in various social settings. The adult professionals lend legitimation to the process. The changes can become self-reinforcing, making it more difficult to reverse course later on if one should desire to do so. Also, as more young children start on the transgender pathway, this tends "to encourage persons to view other persons (especially children) who do not engage in normative sex-role behavior as potential trans[gender persons]." *10 So, children who deviate from patriarchal gender roles may be misguided by adults. Instead of learning more about Patriarchy and its constrictive and oppressive gender roles, children may be encouraged by adults to get on the transgender pathway. Nonconforming children may be misguided into deliberately embarking on social transitioning and also into making their new gender expression conform to their chosen gender's stereotypical patriarchal gender role.

Many young children are deciding that they are transgender and that their "true gender identity," and hence "true sex," are the opposite of their physical sex. How can young children reach that decision? Everyone is immersed in Patriarchy from their births. Everyone is immersed in a patriarchal culture and society from their births. Patriarchy distorts the development of both males and females from their births—as "the coercive power of sex-role socialization is filtered through all institutions in a patriarchal society." *11 Patriarchy is a "social totality." Young children only know life in a patriarchal society. Children are way too young to understand how human civilization is organized by Patriarchy. Young children do not have the education, maturity, and the intellectual tools to critique and deconstruct patriarchal gender roles. If it is difficult for an adult to navigate through a patriarchal society—how much more difficult is it for a child when the child has no understanding of the big-picture historical context of Patriarchy?

Many transgender people rely on, and are dependent on, the patriarchal medical-pharmaceutical industry for medical interventions—namely steps 2-4 of the transgender pathway of puberty blockers, cross-sex hormone treatments, and various surgeries. Since "children cannot provide legal consent to medical treatment of any kind," adults must be involved in making the decisions for medical interventions for children.

There is some question over whether these medical interventions for transgender children (steps 2 & 3) are "essential" or merely "cosmetic." On the one hand, transgender activists strongly affirm the right of every individual to decide their "true gender identity" without any regard or correspondence to their biological sex and physical body. So a transgender person's physical body does not need to correspond in any way with one's chosen gender identity and "true sex." So why would these medical interventions be "essential"? On the other hand, transgender activists argue that puberty blockers and cross-sex hormone treatments are necessary and essential treatments for transgender children. Transgender activists argue that these medical interventions help transgender children to "self-determine their identities at an early age" and assist them in "living their truth." Furthermore, legislation by the political right to prevent these medical interventions for children would "criminalize the healthcare they need to survive." *12 So, one might conclude that these medical interventions are both nonessential and absolutely essential. How can this be? It basically comes down to the medical interventions being "essential" to buttress children's choices of gender identity and to support their fragile mental health which, in turn, affects their physical health.

The second step on the transgender pathway is the medical intervention of using "puberty blockers." This involves taking puberty-suppressing drugs.

> "Blockers are sometimes prescribed to transgender children or youth in order to delay puberty and all the complications it can bring when your body starts doing things that clash with who you know you are." *13 Lee Airton

The step of using puberty blockers is, of course, a step only for children. The prescribing of puberty blockers has been described by trans activists as "hitting a pause" on biological development. It delays or stops physical changes during puberty that transgender children have not chosen for themselves but rather would be "imposed upon them" by their own bodies. But the word "pause" is misleading because time and biological development of one sort or another does not stop for any child. It is also claimed by trans activists that the treatment of puberty blockers is "reversible" if a child should decide to stop it.

> "The claim for the reversibility of puberty-blocking treatment is purely speculative, and it is also inherently misleading, for in developmental biology 'it makes little sense to describe anything as 'reversible' '....virtually every part of the body undergoes significant development in sex-specific ways during puberty, and going through the process at age eighteen can't reverse ten years of blocking it." *14 Ryan T. Anderson

The third step on the transgender pathway is the medical intervention of cross-sex hormone treatments.

> "Hormone replacement therapy, or HRT...alters the body's balance of sex hormones—estrogen for male-to-female and testosterone for female-to-male transitions. Sometimes, male-to-female patients will also be given progesterone, another steroid typically produced by the ovaries, as well as a testosterone blocker, such as spironolactone....the younger a patient starts hormones, typically the better they work." *15 Meeri Kim

Are cross-sex hormone treatments in the best long-term interests of children? Cross-sex hormone treatments intentionally disrupt children's natural internal biological development in order to yield to external control, via the medical industry, and redirect biological development in an unnatural direction. Cross-sex hormone treatments interfere with "the whole body"—the body's complex and integrated systems for males or females. Intuitively, such medical manipulations of children's biological development could have some long-term adverse side-effects. Intuitively, yielding one's growing, vulnerable, and healthy body to external manipulation results in more "disempowerment" rather then "internal empowerment."

The fourth step on the transgender pathway, of various surgeries, is for adults only. Only a minority of transgender people will undergo these surgeries and become "transsexuals." The surgeries represent a further, and troubling, step on the transgender pathway. The surgeries represent serious, and oftentimes major, medical interventions on "healthy" people.

Surgeries on the reproductive organs to go from male-to-female, or from female-to-male, used to be called "sex reassignment" surgeries. That terminology is based on biological sex. Now they are called "gender-affirming" surgeries which is based on an individual's chosen "gender identity." Surgeries can involve primary and secondary sex characteristics. And then there can be continuing minor cosmetic or reconstructive surgeries to reshape other parts of the body.

The molding of transsexual bodies has its origins in Patriarchy. The patriarchal medical-pharmaceutical industry began surgically constructing male-to-female transsexuals in the mid-20th century. One might surmise that some male privilege was involved back then as some men utilized the male top-heavy medical system to become male-to-female transsexuals. The patriarchal technology extended patriarchal medical dominance and male dominion and intruded into and weakened the "female domain": the biological, social, and political space of women on the underside of Patriarchy. (One might ask—what is a *real* woman? Is there anything unique about being *female*? Can any male simply choose to become a female?) As the medical system improved its mastery over various parts of the body, more women were assimilated into the transsexual molding.

> "Women have been assimilated into the transsexual world, as women are assimilated into other male-defined worlds, institutions, and roles, that is, on men's terms." *16 Janice Raymond

The original idea of changing a male body into a female transsexual reflects a patriarchal mindset. It stems from a mindset of superiority, dominance, and control—over nature and the body. Nature and the body are viewed from a mechanistic perspective—allowing for innumerable interventions on various parts—without regard for "the whole."

> "Biological life is anything but mechanistic. Nature is more flow than fixed. There is a dynamic impulse in nature choreographing the various structures through finely tuned regulatory steps and elaborate processes....How the smallest structures of a single cell, such as the nucleus, mitochondria, and golgi apparatus, can work together in a seamless rhythm baffles the search for mechanistic principles. Nature, as [Steve] Talbot writes, is an 'unbearable wholeness of beings.' The awareness of relational holism was part of the rebirth of science in the twentieth century. Quantum physics disclosed a relational holism through the discovery of wave-particle duality, and biological systems were found to work as complex dynamical wholes." *17 Ilia Delio

With power derived from new mechanistic technology, the unfeeling medical technicians could cut up a healthy body in order to construct a man-made artificial woman. And then assimilate and mold more female-to-male transsexuals.

    The fourth step of the transgender pathway, of various surgeries, reinforces the patriarchal mind-body dichotomy. It is a step of greater alienation from one's natural body. One's natural body is subordinated to one's mind and chosen gender to the extent that one willingly undergoes painful surgeries and mutilations of one's natural body. The patriarchal mind-body dichotomy becomes further entrenched since the surgeries are irreversible and the consequences are lifelong.

    Transgender people, and especially transsexuals, are in a way saying "no" to evolutionary biology. They are saying "no" to how human beings have historically evolved and arrived at their current physical bodies. They are saying "no" to the truism that human beings are deeply rooted and belong in their natural habitat and in their natural bodies. They are trying to override evolutionary biology by remaking and redeveloping their bodies through the external manipulations of the patriarchal medical-pharmaceutical industry. However, they are underestimating the enduring strength of evolutionary biology.

While the various surgeries for transsexuals are called "gender-affirming," they do not change the underlying reality of one's biological sex. Biologically, it is impossible for a man or woman to be changed into the opposite sex. One's sex is established at the chromosomal level and during fetal formation. One's whole body and anatomy usually develop organically on that basis for many years before any transgender medical intervention (except when parents decide on questionable early surgeries to reshape their babies based on "abnormalities"). Medical surgeries for transsexuals can remove body parts and do reconstruction work but cannot re-engineer the whole body. For transsexuals, one's "true gender identity," representing one's "true sex," never matches up completely with one's chosen sex—no matter how many medical interventions are employed. The various surgeries taken to try to conform to the body shape and anatomy of their chosen sex will likely result in a lifetime of dependence on the patriarchal medical-pharmaceutical industry for cross-sex hormone treatments, additional cosmetic surgeries, and treatments for iatrogenic complications and side-effects.

For transsexuals, one's "true gender identity" also never matches up with the real life experiences, both physically and mentally, with someone of their chosen sex. They have no real whole, *embodied* experience of their chosen sex. For example, a male-to-female transsexual has no experience of growing up female (24/7) in a patriarchal society, of being a girl disadvantaged in family life with regards to female subordination, including experiencing: unequal access to family resources, unequal household labor expectations, restrictions on outdoor activities, and restricted educational and job opportunities. Male-to-female transsexuals lack experience of patriarchal sexual harassment of females, patriarchal bullying and preying on females, getting sexually assaulted in a female body, and the daily pressures and stresses of childcare and finding adequate resources for raising children. They lack the experience of female puberty, menstruation, sexuality, pregnancy, childbirth, biological motherhood, menopause, etc. Mentally, they have no experience of relating to female body concerns, female fears, female strategies for security, female fantasies, and female dreams and visions for the future. A transsexual will always have this enormous experiential disconnect from their chosen sex.

When a transsexual, who was born a male and then surgically altered to closely resemble a female, says, "I am a woman," they are not only affirming their chosen gender identity. They are expecting affirmation and confirmation from society.

> "Transsexualism urges us to collude in the falsification of reality....Unlike impersonators, transsexuals are not participating in a performance in which the audience suspends disbelief for the duration of the show. They purport to be the real thing. And our suspension of disbelief in their synthetic nature is required as a moral imperative." *18 Janice Raymond

It can be helpful to recognize what one can control and what one can't control. Everyone has free will and the freedom to self-identify as they choose. That is a freedom that transgender people cherish. But one cannot control the degree to which other people will affirm and accommodate one's personal choices. A trans person may seek out affirmation and support from family, friends, allies, a supportive social network, and even from patriarchal society. But achieving full acceptance of transgender positions and rights in a patriarchal society is a contradiction and a mirage since Patriarchy is based on inequality and injustice. Also, one may often exercise a lot of control over one's own body — another cherished freedom. But much of a body's biological development occurs *naturally*—without a person's consent. Seeking to override natural development via medical interventions is not totally in one's control and ultimately is never complete. This is particularly true for trans youth who need adult collaborators for medical interventions. Therefore, a trans person's expectations for outside affirmations, medical interventions, and bodily transformation may need to be repeatedly adjusted based on what they can and can't control— and based on their social context within a heterosexist patriarchal society.

Various gender identity expressions may destabilize patriarchal stereotypes and heterosexual orthodoxy. However, the various gender identities can also obfuscate critiques of Patriarchy and dialogues around transgender accommodations to Patriarchy. Since the transgender-affirmative culture demands acceptance of all options this means that oppressive patriarchal gender roles of "masculine" and "feminine" are also accepted.

The transgender-affirmative culture and the transgender pathway, as a whole, do not represent a real alternative to Patriarchy or any strong resistance to it.

Transgender people are beset with a mental health crisis. Depression and suicidality are extraordinarily high.

"About half of young trans and nonbinary youth in the U.S. seriously contemplated suicide in the past year [2022], as a record-breaking number of bills restricting the rights of LGBTQ people — especially transgender youth — are enacted in state legislatures across the country....That's according to the fifth annual survey on the mental health of LGBTQ young people living in the U.S. released by The Trevor Project, the nation's leading suicide and crisis organization for LGBTQ youth....'As the existence of LGBTQ young people continues to be unfairly put up for debate, it's critical to consistently underscore that these challenges are not inherent to LGBTQ identity, but rather stem from stigma, discrimination, and violence,' [Ronita] Nath said." *19 Muri Assuncao

A toxic, heterosexist, patriarchal culture cultivates prejudices and harmful practices towards sexual minorities. As a result, the social stress on trans youth is very high. The political right is amping up the pressure by using the state's bullying power of laws, coercion, repression, and punishment. Certainly trans youth need lots of help. Certainly trans youth need "safe places" to be shielded from harassment, verbal abuse, and physical harm, and to receive collective emotional support for their personal wounds and daily struggles. Both trans youth and trans adults deserve to be treated with respect, love, and humility. There is always a need for resistance to patriarchal culture, solidarity with the oppressed, and a vision for universal liberation.

<u>Jesus and the Discipleship/Liberation Movement</u>

If a person's goals in life include working and contributing to overcoming Patriarchy, then that will be a very difficult and challenging undertaking. Patriarchy rules human civilizations and is a "social totality." The very popular paths of reforming Patriarchy and seeking to be assimilated and integrated more deeply into a patriarchal society are ineffective and, in the long run, a dead end.

Partially countercultural pathways will always be ineffective in radically transforming a patriarchal society. Jesus offers a different pathway. Jesus calls people to "come out" of patriarchal societies, to form small discipleship groups, households, and communities, and to take up the mission to overcome Patriarchy and to save humanity and the world. Jesus and his discipleship/liberation movement represent humanity's only true hope for succeeding in this mission.

Deep commitment to Jesus and to the path of discipleship is meant to bring about deep resistance to Patriarchy. However, shallow or misguided faith in Jesus, as is abundantly evident all around the world, means most Christians strongly support Patriarchy in many ways. And so Jesus is always in need—not of more people who simply identify as "Christian" but of more deeply-committed followers and disciples.

Jesus calls people to "come out" of Patriarchy and to enter into a closer union with God.

> "One of the scribes came near and heard them disputing with one another, and seeing that he answered them well, he asked him, 'Which commandment is the first of all?' Jesus answered, 'The first is, 'Hear, O Israel: the Lord our God, the Lord is one; you shall love the Lord your God with all your heart, and with all your soul, and with all your mind, and with all your strength.' The second is this, 'You shall love your neighbor as yourself.' There is no other commandment greater than these.'" (Mark12:28-31)

It is God's will that people should love God holistically and "love your neighbor as yourself." Through following Jesus and doing God's will Jesus offers a powerful (Spirit-empowered) and holistic alternative to patriarchal society based on love, nonviolence, and Spirit-power.

To those who follow Jesus, Jesus offers holistic healing and wellness. Jesus "brings about wholeness." Jesus' holistic healing brings about oneness, and unity of spirit, mind, and body. The deepest healing brings harmony of spirit, mind, and body—leading people to prioritize spiritual guidance, self-discipline, and loving service to others. Deep healing brings about reconciliation with God and with all of God's natural creation, i.e., true wholeness. Loving oneself and overcoming the patriarchal mind-body dichotomy means developing spiritual practices, accepting one's body, accepting one's biological sex, caring for one's body, getting healthy physical exercise, eating a healthy diet, developing one's mind and intellect through putting on "the mind of Christ," and following Jesus. Self-love of this sort helps to build self-acceptance, self-esteem, self-confidence, and empathy and love for others.

Loving God, oneself, and all people, also means loving and caring for God's natural creation. Humans are inseparably connected to nature. Human liberation is connected to the liberation of nature, including other living species, from the desecrations of patriarchal civilizations. Human liberation is not the all-in-all. It is an important part of the holistic mission of supporting an Earth-wide New Creation.

Footnotes

1. Lee Airton, PhD; <u>Gender: Your Guide, A Gender-Friendly Primer on What to Know, What to Say, and What to Do in the New Gender Culture</u>; Adams Media, Simon & Schuster, Inc.; Avon, Massachusetts; 2018, p. 54.
2. Madeleine Davison, <u>National Catholic Reporter</u>, "Two Catholic bishops assure transgender people: 'God resides in you,'" April 16-29, 2021.
3. Liz Navratil, <u>Star Tribune</u>, "Mpls. bans conversion therapy," November 24, 2019.
4. Lee Airton, p. 24.
5. David Crary, AP, "Pressure mounts to curtail surgery on intersex kids," <u>Star Tribune</u>, July 26, 2017.
6. David French, NY Times, "Why sex still matters — in sports and law," <u>Star Tribune</u>, June 27, 2023.
7. Lee Airton, p.191.
8. Ryan T. Anderson, <u>When Harry Became Sally: Responding to the Transgender Moment</u>, Encounter Books, New York, 2018, p. 68. This book is banned by Amazon. The political right has a thorough, well-developed critique of the transgender pathway to go along with their coercive and oppressive legislative agenda.
9. Lee Airton, pp. 98-99.
10. Janice Raymond, <u>The Transsexual Empire: The Making of the She-Male</u>, Teachers College Press, Colombia University, New York & London, 1979, 1994, p. xvii. This book is out of print.
11. Janice Raymond, p. 134.

12. These quotes are from trans activists from a radio program on MPR - Minnesota Public Radio.
13. Lee Airton, p. 82.
14. Ryan T. Anderson, pp. 128 &122.
15. Meeri Kim, Washington Post, "Hormone therapy could take years," Star Tribune, August 23, 2013.
16. Janice Raymond, p. 27.
17. Ilia Delio, Re-Enchanting the Earth: Why AI Needs Religion, Orbis Books, Maryknoll, New York, 2020, pp. xiii-xiv.
18. Janice Raymond, p. xxiii.
19. Muri Assuncao, NY Daily News, "Survey: Half of trans, nonbinary youth considered suicide," Duluth News Tribune, May 3, 2023.

Chapter 6

The Patriarchal Medical-Pharmaceutical Industry and the Drug and Alcohol Culture

The big-picture context for every problem, issue, or topic is a very broad understanding of Patriarchy. The basic premise of Patriarchy is male dominance and female subordination, resulting in hierarchy, inequality, oppression, and violence. Patriarchal societies standardize and institutionalize hierarchy, inequality, oppression, and violence.

This chapter will focus mostly on the U.S. Because the topics are so broad this chapter will give only a brief appraisal of the many relevant issues. The general topic is "health"—which is based on "wholeness." However, Patriarchy "fragments the whole," bringing separations and divisions. Patriarchy fragments Earth's one human family, brings divisions between males and females and between many other groups, brings separation between humans and nature, brings separation of mind from body, and brings separation between humans and God. So this chapter is really more about the unhealthy conditions of a patriarchal society and the problems of a healthcare system shaped by Patriarchy.

This chapter will describe how the patriarchal medical-pharmaceutical industry, along with the drug and alcohol culture, serve as *complementary* parts to the patriarchal industrial age, to the fossil-fuel era, to the exploitation of resources to maximize material wealth, to the depopulation of rural areas and the growth of vast urban centers, to growing pollution and waste, and to people's growing faith in new and more complex technology. The patriarchal medical-pharmaceutical industry, along with the drug and alcohol culture, are medicating and drugging humanity as humanity unwittingly stumbles inexorably down "the patriarchal path of ecological ruin."

The patriarchal medical-pharmaceutical industry in the U.S. has its roots, of course, in Patriarchy. It began with very strong sex and racial (white-supremacist) biases resulting in systemic problems. It began with exclusively white-male physicians. As in many other professions women were excluded at the beginning of the profession. Some medical educational institutions had an association with slavery and procured cadavers, without consent, from among people of color. Male physicians learned to dissect the body and figure out ways to treat various parts. Since the "domain" of the medical industry is the human body, and since the industry was (and is) patriarchal, the industry increased male dominance over female bodies. Women and girls have often been passive patients injected with experimental drugs, undergone unnecessary surgeries, been subjected to coercive sterilizations, and have grown dependent on the patriarchal industry from birth to death.

The medical-pharmaceutical industry developed from a patriarchal mindset of domination, objectification, and fragmentation.

> "The mechanical approach to medicine has dominated the health care profession for the past 200 years. British health expert Thomas McKeown sums up the prevalent attitude: 'The approach to biology and medicine established during the seventeenth century was an engineering one based on a physical model. Nature was conceived in mechanistic terms, which led biology to the idea that a living organism could be regarded as a machine which might be taken apart and reassembled if its structure and function were fully understood. In medicine, the same concept led further to the belief that an understanding of disease processes and of the body's response to them would make it possible to intervene therapeutically, mainly by physical (surgery), chemical or electrical methods.'" *1 Jeremy Rifkin with Ted Howard

Missing from this patriarchal mindset was a holistic perspective, the connection of humans with nature, and the importance of people actively participating in their own healing. Knowledge, expertise, technology, and medications were in the hands of doctors and the pharmaceutical industry.

In general, medical research has focused mainly on white males. This has resulted in medical "knowledge gaps" and "credibility gaps" for females and people of color. For example:

> "The US Nuclear Regulatory Commission's archaic and grossly biased standard called 'Reference Man' estimates

health risks from ionizing radiation based on a male who is
'20 to 30 years old, weighs 154 pounds, is 5-foot and 6
inches tall, and is Caucasian with a Western European or
North American lifestyle' — a reference nothing like the
profile of the most vulnerable — girls under five. [Mary]
Olson's work demonstrates that 'Reference Man' exposes
girls and young women to dangerously high radiation, 'not
just from nuclear warfare but also from more routine
radiation exposures like CT scans, air travel, and medical
x-rays.'" *2 Nukewatch

A general medical bias against females has also resulted in a "credibility gap" where medical professionals often don't believe women and where women's pain and symptoms are often dismissed or are treated with skepticism. This often results in undiagnosed or misdiagnosed health problems and, in time, greater health complications. Women's health problems like heart disease, endometriosis, or ovarian cancer are often given lower priority than male health problems. Black women still experience extraordinarily high maternal death rates.

"The National Center for Health Statistics reports that in
2020, the maternal mortality rate for Black women was
55.3 deaths per 100,000 live births. The 2020 rate for
white women was 19.1 deaths per 100,000 live births.
Black women are also more likely to have C-sections,
have their pain minimized or ignored, report mistreatment,
and have stillbirths than white women....the grim statistics
are often a result of a health care system that leaves Black
mothers to fend for themselves. 'Racial and ethnic
inequities in obstetrics and gynecology cannot be
reversed without addressing all aspects of racism and
racial bias, including sociopolitical forces that perpetuate
racism,' the American College of Obstetricians and
Gynecologists said in a statement last year [2022]." *3
Erica L. Green

While much medical research has focused on white males, some unethical medical research has been done on people at the bottom of patriarchal hierarchies. For example, the "Tuskegee Study" was conducted by the U.S. Public Health Service from 1932-1972 with Black men with syphilis.

"For four decades, the U.S. government had denied
hundreds of poor Black men treatment for syphilis so
researchers could study its ravages on the
body....Researchers told them they were to be treated for

'bad blood,' a catchall term used to describe several ailments, including anemia, fatigue and syphilis. Treatment then consisted mostly of doses of arsenic and mercury....Eventually, more than 600 men were enrolled. What they were not told was that about a third would receive no treatment at all—even after penicillin became available in the 1940s." *4 Allen G. Breed

Another example of unethical medical research used prisoners.

"More than 50 years ago [1971], nearly a dozen men incarcerated outside of Philadelphia enrolled in an experiment funded by Johnson & Johnson....In one study, inmates were paid to be injected with potentially cancer-causing asbestos so the company could compare its effects on their skin vs. that of talc, a key component in its iconic baby powder. University of Pennsylvania dermatologist Albert Kligman conducted hundreds of human experiments over two decades at Holmesburg Prison in Pennsylvania. The testing regime, funded by entities such as Dow Chemical and the U.S. government, involved mostly Black inmates....J & J's involvement in the talc studies hasn't been made public before now....J & J officials said they regretted the firm's involvement with the dermatologist. Still, they noted the tests didn't violate research standards at the time." *5 Jef Feeley

Importantly, the implied acceptable "research standards at the time" were not subject to public transparency and J & J's talc studies on prisoners remained a secret until they became public through court litigation in 2021.

Despite the patriarchal medical-pharmaceutical industry having many "dark secrets," past and present, it still has great credibility with the public. The industry works to provide individual remedies for almost all health problems. The industry focuses on individuals and largely ignores the larger context of families, communities, environment, and society. The industry treats individuals with very serious and potentially lethal health problems and helps to put most people on the road to improved health. Diagnostic testing and machinery help to provide lots of information and data about individuals' health problems. So the public keeps returning to the industry for medical assistance. Yet despite the industry helping out large numbers of people, the industry also has inherent and intractable problems—and needs to be viewed within a big-picture context.

Environmental Decline and Ill Health

The patriarchal medical-pharmaceutical industry is a complementary part of a patriarchal society. A patriarchal society, in varying degrees, generates ill-health, sickness, and disease. The patriarchal medical-pharmaceutical industry patches up individuals and prescribes drugs so that people can return to an unhealthy society. This sickness to medical treatment to sickness loop rarely gets to the roots of health problems stemming from a patriarchal society.

> "Seemingly, the more we invest in our health care system, the less healthy we become....the main reason is that we embrace an inaccurate narrative about health and health care. We consider health to be an individual, not a community, responsibility and consider treatment more important than prevention. We fail to recognize that only about 10% of our health is determined by health care and 30% by individual behavior choices while 60% is determined by community factors — social, economic and environmental conditions." *6 Edward P. Ehlinger

A key contextual point is that most of health is determined by community and not individual factors.

> "For more than a century, analysis of disease trends has shown that the environment is the primary determinant of the state of general health of any population." *7 Ivan Illich

A patriarchal, capitalist economic system *speeds up* the exploitation of natural resources and thereby harms the environment on which human health is dependent upon. Harmful climate change/chaos is a consequence.

> "Across the planet, animals—and the diseases they carry—are shifting to accommodate a globe on the fritz. And they're not alone: ticks, mosquitoes, bacteria, algae, even fungi are on the move, shifting or expanding their historical ranges to adapt to climatic conditions that are evolving at an unprecedented pace. These changes are not happening in a vacuum. Deforestation, mining, agriculture, and urban sprawl are taking bites out of the globe's remaining wild areas, contributing to biodiversity loss that's occurring at a rate unprecedented in human history....Climate change displaces some 20 million people every year—people who need housing, medical care, food and other essentials that put strain on already

fragile systems. All of these factors create conditions ripe for human illness." *8 Zoya Teirstein

A patriarchal society and how it is organized is a key factor in the overall health, or ill-health, of a community. Populations are getting more concentrated in urban centers and further distanced from nature. Large metropolises are dependent upon an exploitive, colonizing economic system which keeps resources flowing from rural areas to urban areas. Large cities are highly dependent upon a large-scale transfer of resources from rural areas—of energy, food, and labor. And the technology and methods used to extract large agricultural surpluses for cities —one-crop farming, heavy use of inorganic fertilizers and pesticides, energy-guzzling machinery, over-use of aquifers, draining of wetlands, and farming on marginal lands—also results in serious ecological harm and pollution.

The patriarchal capitalist economic system and the urban and suburban architecture of housing and transportation work to fragment and atomize the population. These structures support individualistic jobs, cars, and housing units. They assist in the segregation of people which contributes to the oppression of poor people. Poor people are over-concentrated in undesirable locations, face high rental housing costs, often live in sub-standard housing, and face the threat and oftentimes the reality of homelessness. The high concentration of people into small urban areas which have great economic inequalities and where large amounts of air pollution and waste are generated negatively affects health. It results in more anti-social behavior, neurosis, and illness. Additionally, urban crime, assaults, violence, stress, and PTSD (post-traumatic stress disorder) contribute to poor health.

The whole world continues a trend toward greater separation from nature through greater urbanization. This does not bode well for people's health. The United Nations' Intergovernmental Panel on Climate Change recently issued a report that found that:
> "The world's cities are a big driver of planet-warming emissions....'The 21st-century will be the urban century, defined by a massive increase in global urban populations,' the report said. About 55% of the world's population lived in cities in 2018, a figure expected to jump to 68% by 2050....Cities in 2020 were responsible

for up to 72% of global greenhouse gas emissions, up from 62% in 2015." *9 Daniel Trotta

Greater urbanization and worsening climate change are pushing humanity towards a dystopian future.

In the U.S., due to a long history of white supremacy and racism, the negative health effects from pollution and waste disproportionately fall upon people of color. "Environmental racism" results in many people of color living in close proximity to polluting industries.

"The racial composition of a community is the single variable best able to explain the existence or nonexistence of commercial hazardous waste facilities in that area. Racial minorities, primarily African Americans and Hispanics, are strikingly overrepresented in communities with such facilities." *10 Charles Lee

Historically, large racial communities were deliberately segregated and polluting industries were intentionally located close to them.

Decades of federal housing discrimination did not only depress home values, lower job opportunities and spur poverty in communities deemed undesirable because of race. It's why 45 million Americans are breathing dirtier air today, according to a landmark study released [3-9-2022]. The practice known as redlining was outlawed more than a half-century ago, but it continues to impact people who live in neighborhoods that government mortgage officers shunned for 30 years because people of color and immigrants lived in them….Throughout redlining's history, local zoning officials worked with businesses to place polluting operations such as industrial plants, major roadways and shipping ports in and around neighborhoods that the federal government marginalized….'This groundbreaking study builds on the solid empirical evidence that systemic racism is killing and making people of color sick, it's just that simple,' said Robert Bullard." *11 Darryl Fears

<u>The Growing Dominance of the Patriarchal Medical-Pharmaceutical Industry</u>

The patriarchal medical-pharmaceutical industry is a complementary part of a patriarchal society. The industry has grown in dominance and has diminished lower-cost alternatives.

"Our health care system is organized around a single type of professional — physicians. This increases costs and limits the ability of non-physicians to provide care at the highest level of their training and abilities. Midwife-run birth centers, for example, have excellent birth outcomes at lower cost and higher patient satisfaction but are limited by restrictive systems and policies. Advanced practice nurses, community health workers, doulas, nutritionists, social workers, etc., are also systematically underutilized and often actively opposed by the medical establishment, despite solid evidence of their value, especially in underserved communities." *12 Edward P. Ehlinger

As the patriarchal medical-pharmaceutical industry has become more dominant, people have become more dependent upon it. The very high costs of hospitalization, doctor visits, medical tests, and medications make healthcare unaffordable without health insurance. So, dependency upon the industry leads directly to dependency on health insurance. And the costs of health insurance keep going up, leaving many people underinsured. This leads to the problem of burdensome healthcare debt.

"An estimated 100 million people in the U.S., or 41% of all adults, have health care debt, compared with 42 million who have student debt." *13 Elisabeth Rosenthal

Many hospitals have contributed to this debt burden by shirking their charitable responsibilities.

"More than half of the roughly 5,000 hospitals in the United States are nonprofits. In exchange for avoiding taxes, the IRS requires them to offer services, such as free health care for low-income patients, that help their communities. But the [New York] Times this year [2022] has documented how large chains of nonprofit hospitals have moved away from their charitable missions. Some have skimped on free care for the poor, illegally saddling tens of thousands of patients with debts." *14 Rebecca Robbins, Katie Thomas, Jessica Silver-Greenberg

This burdensome healthcare debt-load adds stress to daily life and is itself unhealthy.

As the patriarchal medical-pharmaceutical industry has become more dominant, people have become more disempowered. New technology keeps leading to newer and more expensive medical machinery. To pay for the very expensive machinery it needs to get a lot of use. This contributes to over-diagnosis and more unnecessary tests and surgeries. Patients become more dependent on doctors and their medical machines.

> "Western faith in medical progress has reached the point where people accept, without criticism, that past technological problems need more technological solutions, which can themselves turn into problems. This is the height of technological determinism, and women are left with an increased dependency on more and more questionable technical solutions....
> Opposition to these [new reproductive] technologies is based on the more political feminist perspective that *women as a class have a stake in reclaiming the female body, not as female nature, but by refusing to yield control of it to men, to the fetus, to the state, and most recently to those liberals who advocate that women control our bodies by giving up control."* *15 Janice Raymond

Patriarchal "medical progress" often means women, as well as men, become more dependent upon the industry and more disempowered.

New technologies need to be questioned as to who benefits and who is disempowered. No technology is "neutral." It always has a big-picture context—such as a very broad understanding of Patriarchy. New technological advancements are relentless.

> "Current scientific developments and expectations in the fields of genetics, robotics, nanotechnology, information science, artificial intelligence, evolutionary biology, and neuroscience are raising unprecedented ethical and theological questions about the direction in which we—and life on earth along with us—may be heading....New scientific ideas and techniques are opening up the prospect of radically tailoring what it means to be human, not only socially and culturally but also physically and cognitively—a process now referred to as *transhumanism."* *16 John F. Haught

New technology gets filtered through a patriarchal society and patriarchal institutions. New technology in the hands of the state, the military, police forces, large corporations, the rich and powerful, and the medical industry can potentially be incredibly harmful to many people. New warnings about unregulated A.I.

have stated that it could possibly bring humanity closer to extinction.

     The patriarchal medical-pharmaceutical industry's dominance elevates the power of doctors over patients, putting many people in a vulnerable position where abuses can easily occur. Sexual abuses can happen to patients of any age—even the young and physically strong.

> "Hundreds of female gymnasts who were sexually abused by Larry Nassar, a former team doctor of the national gymnastics team, have agreed to a $380 million settlement with USA Gymnastics and the U.S. Olympic & Paralympic Committee, ending the latest dark chapter in one of the biggest molestation cases in sports history....Gymnasts have battled anxiety, depression and post-traumatic stress disorder, and some girls and women have attempted suicide because of Nassar's abuse, which he perpetrated under the guise of medical treatment." 17 Juliet Macur

How could Nassar abuse so many girls and women over a period of years—when people in positions of authority were aware that abuses were occurring?

> "In 2019, a U.S. Senate report on Nassar found that officials from the U.S. Olympic & Paralympic Committee, USA Gymnastics, Michigan State University and the FBI 'sat on evidence of his sexual misconduct for over a year — allowing for the additional sexual abuse of dozens of other girls.'" *18 Juliet Macur, Michael Levenson

Various patriarchal institutions were reluctant to act on reports of sexual abuse, allowing for more girls and women to be abused. These particular institutions are representative of a wider problem.

> "The University of California will pay $243.6 million to settle allegations that hundreds of women were sexually abused by a former UCLA gynecologist…by Dr. James Heaps over a 35-year career....The lawsuits said UCLA ignored decades of complaints and deliberately concealed abuse." *19 Star Tribune

> "Columbia University and its affiliated hospitals on Friday announced a $165 million settlement with 147 patients of a former gynecologist accused of sexual abuse by dozens of women." *20 Star Tribune

The above examples would seem to indicate that medical sexual abuse is widespread - and that it often takes a "critical mass" of complaints and a lawsuit for patriarchal institutions to take these complaints seriously.

The patriarchal medical-pharmaceutical industry's dominance becomes more oppressive when it partners on a decision-making level with the patriarchal state. The state can legitimize and elevate a narrow-minded medical model for addressing some key health problems.

> "The medical model....serves as the 'new theology' for the therapeutic and medical priests....an approach to human conflicts from a diagnostic and disease perspective to be solved by specialized technical and professional experts....
> Today especially, it is no longer the alliance of church and state that should be feared, that is, *theocracy*, but rather the alliance between medicine and the state, that is, *pharmacracy*. It is medicine that presently functions as the new secular religion, with the continuous aid of sustained government support." *21 Janice Raymond

When the state partners with the medical industry the opinions of "medical experts" are elevated above everyone else's, a moralizing and self-righteous medical agenda is heavily promoted, and the state weighs in with its coercive power. State-backed medical mandates, lockdowns, and increased policing of individuals prioritize a "medical-industry solution" while ostracizing any dissent or resistance.

> "Diagnosis always intensifies stress, defines incapacity, imposes inactivity, and focuses apprehension on non-recovery, on uncertainty, and on one's dependence upon future medical findings, all of which amounts to a loss of autonomy for self-definition. It also isolates a person in a special role, separates him [or her] from the normal and healthy, and requires submission to the authority of specialized personnel. Once a society organizes for a preventive disease-hunt, it gives epidemic proportions to diagnosis. This ultimate triumph of the therapeutic culture turns the independence of the average healthy person into an intolerable form of deviance." *22 Ivan Illich

While helping lots of sick and/or injured people, the behemoth patriarchal medical-pharmaceutical industry is also responsible for large numbers of harmful iatrogenic events. Medical iatrogenic disorders are harmful events unintentionally caused by doctors, hospital staff, medical machinery, and prescription drugs.

> "Too much money ($3.6 trillion per year) is spent on medical care (less than 3% going to prevention) with many treatments doing more harm than good. Approximately 25% of total health care costs are spent on wasteful activities and about 250,000 deaths per year are due to medical errors, making 'iatrogenic' conditions the third leading cause of death." *23 Edward P. Ehlinger

There is currently no national annual count of medical errors, drug-related miscues and harmful side-effects, and medical- and hospital-derived infections that result in patient deaths. The 250,000 iatrogenic deaths per year is an estimate based on research and various studies and could very well be an undercount. Some of the infections that result in deaths from sepsis are due to medical iatrogenesis.

> "Sepsis is the body's out-of-control reaction to an infection....Sepsis strikes more than 1.5 million people in the United States each year and kills more than 250,000." *24 Lauran Neergaard

Many medical devices are a cause of iatrogenesis.
> "In hospitals around the world, the snakelike duodenoscope is regarded as an indispensable tool for diagnosing and treating diseases of the pancreas and bile ducts....Tests...found that 1 in 20 duodenoscopes retained disease-causing microbes like E. coli even after proper cleaning....The alternative to the device is open surgery, which carries its own risks, said Dr. Bret Petersen, a gastroenterologist at Mayo Clinic in Rochester, Minn. But the inability to properly clean the instrument between patients has proved to be its 'Achilles heel,' he said." *25 Roni Caryn Rabin

Many medical devices have to be recalled and/or discontinued.
> "After years of advocacy by injured patients, the U.S. Food and Drug Administration has ordered the makers of mesh devices for the repair of pelvic organ prolapse to remove the products from the U.S. market. The announcement...came after years of scrutiny and well over 100,000 lawsuits from women around the world.... [T]he most commonly reported problems included severe pelvic pain, pain during intercourse, infection, bleeding, organ perforation and urinary problems from mesh eroding into surrounding tissues." *26 Joe Carlson

One might note the "prompt action" of the FDA after over 100,000 lawsuits from women had been filed.

Harmful Effects of Pharmaceutical Drugs

The patriarchal medical-pharmaceutical industry relies very heavily on pharmaceutical drugs. Pharmaceutical drugs offer a quick remedy for health problems—which is desired by patients and doctors alike. Patients' demands for drugs contributes to the overuse of antibiotics and the overprescription of other drugs. A patriarchal society is organized for speed and immediate gratification—and pharmaceutical drugs fit right into that culture whether they are effective or not.

All drugs have side effects, some of which can be very harmful and even lethal. Many drugs have to be taken off the market years after they have done a lot of harm.

The U.S.'s opioid and overdose epidemic can be traced back to the manufacture and sale of very addictive pharmaceutical painkillers.

> "Purdue Pharma…in 1996 introduced the slow-release opioid painkiller OxyContin. Experts trace the epidemic to the appearance of Oxy, its heavy marketing, and its migration into the illicit drug trade along with other opioids….The industry shipped 76 billion oxycodone and hydrocodone pills from 2006 through 2012….The public's search for accountability has centered on Purdue and its owners, the Sackler family. But during the height of the crisis, from 2006 to 2012, Purdue's sales represented only 3% of the market….Prescription opioid overdoses have killed more than 200,000 people in the U.S. since 1996." *27 Joel Achenbach, Lenny Bernstein, Robert O'Harrow Jr., Shawn Boburg

Opioid manufacturers have been sued by state governments and others and have agreed to pay many billions of dollars in settlements.

> "Drugmaker Johnson & Johnson and three major distributors [Amerisource Bergen, Cardinal Health, and McKesson] finalized nationwide settlements over their role in the opioid addiction crisis…an announcement that clears the way for $26 billion to flow to nearly every state and local government in the U.S." *28 Geoff Mulvihill

In a related settlement, Native American tribes will get their own payments.

> "Hundreds of Native American tribes that have suffered disproportionately high addiction and death rates during the opioid epidemic agreed...to a tentative settlement of $590 million with Johnson & Johnson and the country's three largest drug distributors....According to one study, pregnant American Indian women were up to 8.7 times more likely than pregnant women from other groups to be diagnosed with opioid dependency or abuse." *29 Jan Hoffman

The patriarchal medical-pharmaceutical industry helped to fuel an overdose epidemic which is still continuing today, with tragic consequences.

> "More than 107,000 Americans died of drug overdoses last year [2021], setting another tragic record in the nation's escalating overdose epidemic, the Centers for Disease Control and Prevention estimated Wednesday....U.S. overdose deaths have risen most years for more than two decades. The increase began in the 1990s with overdoses involving opioid painkillers, followed by waves of deaths led by other opioids like heroin and—most recently—illicit fentanyl." *30 Mike Stobbe

The patriarchal medical pharmaceutical industry often advertises and convinces the public on the effectiveness of drugs —even when there isn't any solid science behind their claims. Industry promotion of antidepressants, or SSRIs, led to more than 34 million adults taking antidepressants (in 2014). They were being misled.

> "The most popular depression drugs taken by millions don't work by fixing an 'imbalance of the brain's neurotransmitters,' as many drug advertisements claim or imply. That's because depression isn't caused by a chemical imbalance, according to a new analysis published in Molecular Psychiatry....[T]he British Medical Journal [also] did a deep examination of the clinical data....What they found was that the drugs did work better than placebos - but only in about 15% of the patients....the benefits beyond placebo were concentrated in just 15% of patients....The possibility that the majority of patients are feeling better through an

> illusion raises big ethical questions….[Irving] Kirsch says he's concerned that the benefits of SSRIs are often short-lived. The drugs aren't getting at the root of the problem—especially for 85% of patients." *31 Faye Flam

Most antidepressants are addictive, have side effects, and cause difficult withdrawal problems when someone wants to get off the drugs. However, the longer people are taking the drugs the better it is for the drug manufacturers.

The patriarchal pharmaceutical industry is not eco-friendly. It is not in harmony with the natural environment. It is a source of pollution.

> "Potentially toxic levels of pharmaceutical drugs have been found in a quarter of river locations examined across the world, a study found. Researchers from around the world surveyed more than 1,000 sites on 258 rivers….The study, published in the Proceedings of the National Academy of Sciences (PNAS) warns that pollution of the world's rivers by medicinal chemicals is a global problem. Pollution poses a risk to freshwater habitats and wildlife, potentially could contribute to the buildup of antimicrobial resistance, and also threatens global goals on water quality and pollution….The research found lower- and middle-income countries were the most polluted, while rubbish dumping along river banks, inadequate wastewater infrastructure and pharmaceutical manufacturing and dumping of septic tank contents into rivers were the activities most associated with the issue." *32 PA Media/dpa

The Patriarchal Drug and Alcohol Culture

A strong and pervasive drug and alcohol culture is part of patriarchal U.S. culture. Drug and alcohol use are widely promoted throughout society. Drug use is widespread and, as one ages, the number of drugs the elderly take seems to keep increasing. Over-the-counter drugs, prescription drugs, and even illegal drugs are ubiquitous. Alcohol consumption is also aggressively promoted—both for group socializing and for individual in-home use.

Historically, an alcohol culture has been a feature of patriarchal U.S. culture and masculinity. There have also been times of powerful campaigns against alcohol sales and consumption—which have been met with strong opposition from many men. Historically, men in the U.S. were by far the major consumers of alcohol.

> "After the American Revolution, a plentiful supply of cheap untaxed whiskey made from surplus corn on the western frontier caused alcohol consumption to soar. Whiskey cost less than beer, wine, coffee, tea, or milk, and it was safer than water. By the 1820s, the average adult white male drank a half pint of whiskey a day. Liquor corrupted elections, wife beating and child abuse were common, and many crimes were committed while the perpetrator was under the influence." *33 W.J. Rorabaugh

The pervasive alcohol culture affected the patriarchal medical industry.

> "Medical schools included warnings to students, but most physicians in the early 1800s believed that alcohol was an important medicine. Physicians especially favored laudanum, which was opium dissolved in alcohol. Laudanum calmed the nerves and miraculously ended the craving for alcohol. Children's nurses used laudanum to quiet babies." *34 W.J. Rorabaugh

Men were drawn to drink alcohol in all-male saloons. The saloons were not only centers of male-socializing but some became centers for all-male political machines.

> "Muckraking magazines gradually exposed urban corruption practiced by political machines whose power was rooted in saloons." *35 W.J. Rorabaugh

Prior to national prohibition, "New York City alone had thirteen thousand saloons." *36 National prohibition of alcohol sales, using the coercive power of male-run police forces and courts, was certain to fail due to very strong opposition from working-class men and the increase in male-run criminal organizations.

Historically, men have consumed much more alcohol than women—but that is changing, with some significant negative health effects for women.

> "For nearly a century, women have been closing the gender gap in alcohol consumption, binge-drinking and alcohol use disorder. What was previously a 3-1 ratio for risky drinking habits in men vs. women is closer to 1-to-1 globally, a 2016 analysis of several studies suggested. And the latest U.S. data from 2019 shows that women in their teens and early 20s reported drinking and getting

drunk at higher rates than their male peers….This trend parallels the rise in mental health concerns among young women….Research shows women suffer health consequences of alcohol—liver disease, heart disease and cancer—more quickly than men and even at lower levels of consumption." *37 Aneri Pattani

There are many factors in the current patriarchal U.S. culture causing a rise in mental health problems for youth, and disproportionately for girls.

"Celebrity-worshipping and excessively fashion- and beauty-conscious American girls are trying to survive in a junk culture while simultaneously being malnourished, sleep-deprived, over-stressed, over-drugged, over-vaccinated, sexually-harassed, sexually-abused, and screen time- and pornography-toxified all the while trying to pretend to be happy and not emotionally distressed! Impossible!" *38 Gary Kohls

Due to the COVID-19 pandemic, the many world crises, and the general direction of the patriarchal culture, more youth are getting treated by the patriarchal medical-pharmaceutical industry.

"The Centers for Disease Control and Prevention is warning of an accelerating mental health crisis among adolescents, with more than 4 in 10 teens reporting that they feel 'persistently sad or hopeless,' and 1 in 5 saying they have contemplated suicide, according to the results of a survey published [3-31-2022]….The survey results also underscore the particular vulnerability of LGBTQ students, who reported higher rates of suicide attempts and poor mental health. Nearly half of gay, lesbian and bisexual teens said they had contemplated suicide during the pandemic, compared with 14% of their heterosexual peers. Girls, too, reported faring worse than boys. They were twice as likely to report poor mental health. More than 1 in 4 girls reported that they had seriously contemplated attempting suicide during the pandemic, twice the rate of boys. They also reported higher rates of drinking and tobacco use than boys." *39 Moriah Balingit

Putting more youth on prescription drugs for mental health issues does not get to the roots of the problems. Instead, it sets up youth to be lifelong consumers of pharmaceutical drugs.

The patriarchal culture and alcohol industry have targeted and promoted women's alcohol consumption, including consumption by mothers.

"From Facebook, Twitter and Instagram, to movies and store shelves, a ubiquitous narrative has taken hold in popular culture: that it's acceptable, expected and funny for moms to use wine to make it through the day....Because drinking is an accepted practice, it's easy to fall into the habit of using alcohol as a way to de-stress, she [Gabrielle Glaser] said. 'There's anxiety around being a mother,' Glaser said, and 'binge drinking has become completely normalized' as a way to have fun or blow off steam. "That starts in college and carries through to your first job,' she added, and 'it can easily be part of being a mother, as well.'" *40 Kate Thayer

Alcohol consumption by mothers usually comes after close to 9 months of abstinence during pregnancy. Any alcohol consumption during pregnancy can result in Fetal Alcohol Spectrum Disorders in babies. Despite this, the patriarchal culture and alcohol industry promote alcohol consumption by women and mothers.

The COVID-19 pandemic exacerbated existing problems. "A study in JAMA Network Open in 2020 found that the days in which women drank excessively (defined as four or more drinks in a few hours) increased 41% during lockdown. Another report, from RTI International for the National Institute on Alcohol Abuse and Alcoholism, said that mothers with children under 5 increased their drinking by more than 300% during the pandemic. But the pattern of increased alcohol abuse by women appears to have preceded the pandemic....From 2001 to 2013, there was a 58% increase in women's heavy drinking and an 84% increase in alcohol-use disorder....From 1997 to 2017, alcohol-related deaths among women rose by 85%....When I began thinking about sobriety, I knew alcohol could be bad for the liver, but was disturbed to learn that it also attacks the immune systems and is connected with more than 60 different diseases....Recently, the American Cancer Society changed its recommended alcohol intake to zero because of its close association with cancer." *41 Ericka Andersen

The patriarchal drug and alcohol culture supports patriarchal fragmentation. The culture offers a type of social camaraderie and "good spirits and good times." However, overuse of drugs and alcohol results in fractured relationships and ill health. The patriarchal drug and alcohol culture produces many drug addicts and alcoholics. Addictions are a poor replacement for spiritual connections with God. Addicts fill their internal spiritual emptiness with selfish, self-absorbed, self-medicating intoxicants. Eventually, addicts' bodies become dependent upon and demand regular doses of drugs and/or alcohol. There are many negative health consequences.

It has been popular wisdom to think that drinking in moderation has some health benefits. Dr. Michael Criqui, professor emeritus in preventive medicine at the University of California, San Diego, used to think so. However:
> "A 2018 study, which Criqui co-authored, analyzed information from nearly 600 studies across 195 countries to determine the level of alcohol use that minimized harm. The answer: zero. It came as a surprise, he said. 'I can give you no medical justification for drinking,' Criqui said."
> *42 Jenna Ross

Another study, led by University of Pennsylvania researchers suggests that drinking in moderation can be harmful to the brain.
> "People who drank the equivalent of just one daily glass of wine were found to have slightly smaller brains on average, than nondrinkers. The apparent effect from one daily drink was equivalent to two additional years of brain aging for a typical 50-year-old, the authors determined by analyzing MRI scans of more than 36,000 middle-aged people. And the connection grew sharper with more alcohol: On average, the brains of those who consumed two daily drinks looked 10 years older than those of nondrinkers." *43 Star Tribune News Services

Drinking a "nightcap" before going to sleep also has negative effects.
> "How many alcoholic drinks does it take to spoil a good night's sleep?....'The answer is one,' said [Sarah] Moe, founder of Sleep Health Specialists....'Alcohol has a huge impact on sleep,' said Twin Cities sleep medicine physician Dr. Michael Howell....Alcohol has an outsized

impact on our rest because it worsens sleep in many ways. Even a moderate amount of alcohol can disrupt melatonin production; mess with sleep stages, circadian rhythms and your internal clock; make you wake up to use the bathroom; and even trigger or exacerbate disorders like sleep apnea, sleepwalking and insomnia." *44 Erica Pearson

Alcohol consumption can result in a lot of harm, some of which is particularly patriarchal, combining male dominance with male violence.
"Conservative estimates of sexual assault prevalence suggest that 25 percent of American women have experienced sexual assault, including rape.
Approximately one-half of those cases involve alcohol consumption by the perpetrator, victim, or both. Alcohol contributes to sexual assault through multiple pathways, often exacerbating existing risk factors." *45 National Institute on Alcohol Abuse and Alcoholism
Alcohol consumption is often a factor in male sexual assaults of females. Alcohol itself does not cause assaults. However, a heterosexual-male sexual predator may use alcohol and drugs as a gateway to sexually assault women and girls.

Jesus and the Discipleship/Liberation Movement

In these times of multiple world crises, especially climate change/chaos, Earth's 6th great age of mass extinctions, rampant gun violence and militarism, the drug and alcohol culture keeps many people at a "low level of consciousness." This blocks the spiritual progress that is needed to overcome Patriarchy. Spiritual progress involves reversing Patriarchy's "fragmenting the whole" by restoring humanity's connections to God, nature, and all living creatures. A holistic and powerful alternative to Patriarchy is needed—and Jesus and his discipleship/liberation movement are meant to provide it. However, Jesus needs lots more followers and disciples.

Of course, during Jesus' few years of active ministry, nearly 2000 years ago, in a small region of the Middle East, Patriarchy ruled. Most of the Hebrew people were poor and oppressed, living under the rule of the militaristic, slave-based Roman Empire. Poverty was widespread and there was much sickness and suffering.

Jesus offered a holistic revolutionary alternative to living under oppressive, patriarchal Roman rule. Jesus called people to follow him and to live a new life in "God's kingdom or commonwealth" on Earth. Jesus responded to people's suffering, injuries, and diseases by healing many people through God's love and Spirit-power. However, while everyone who needs physical healing wants healing, very few people want to make a big lifestyle change. Most people's vision of life is to find a niche in patriarchal society and just hope for better leaders, reforms, and changes in patriarchal society. But patriarchal society itself is the root cause for most illness, traumatic experiences, and suffering.

Mere physical healing is only one part, albeit large, of holistic healing. Jesus' ministry provided many opportunities for people to experience different levels of healing. For example:
> "And there was a woman who had had a flow of blood for twelve years, and who had suffered much under many physicians, and had spent all that she had, and was no better but rather grew worse. She had heard the reports about Jesus, and came up behind him in the crowd and touched his garment. For she said, 'If I touch even his garment, I shall be made well.' And the hemorrhage ceased; and she felt in her body that she was healed of her disease. And Jesus, perceiving in himself that power had gone forth from him, immediately turned about in the crowd, and said, 'Who touched my garments?' And his disciples said to him, 'You see the crowd pressing around you, and yet you say, "Who touched me?"' And he looked around to see who had done it. But the woman, knowing what had been done to her, came in fear and trembling and fell down before him, and told him the whole truth. And he said to her, 'Daughter, your faith has made you well; go in peace, and be healed of your disease.'" (Mark 5:25-34 Revised Standard Version)

A woman of low status, unnamed and broke, had suffered much in her patriarchal society. Her patriarchal society deemed every woman to be unclean and contagious during menstruation and prescribed isolation during the bleeding period and for seven days afterward, to be followed by a priestly ritual of atonement. Thus women of birthing age spent much of their lives in a cycle of social uncleanness, isolation, and ritual cleansing. The woman in the above passage had a flow of blood for twelve years, making her perpetually unclean and contagious. (Leviticus 15:25-27) The patriarchal healthcare she received took all her money and only increased her suffering. However, an encounter with Jesus provided her with an opportunity for healing. She devised a plan to clandestinely approach and touch Jesus from behind and in the midst of the crowd. This clandestine plan would provide cover for her violating patriarchal social and purity codes. Her faith in Jesus caused her to believe that instead of spreading contagion to Jesus by touching his clothes, she would experience healing power from Jesus. Her plan worked remarkably well until Jesus stopped and brought her action out into the open. The woman's healing was not complete even though she had actively participated in her healing and had made contact with the ultimate source of healing and Spirit-power (Jesus/God). She was still feeling the weight and oppression of patriarchal society. She came forward in fear and trembling, cowering under the punitive judgment of patriarchal society. But Jesus called her forth and gave her a measure of safe space. In a mixture of fear and faith and in front of the whole crowd she spoke her truth of faith in Jesus and of subverting patriarchal purity codes. Jesus responded by lifting up her social position, calling her "daughter" and thereby affirming her valuable place in God's family. Jesus affirmed her faith as being instrumental in her healing, and told her to go in peace—without fear of reprisal or social stigma. Thus the woman, without financial cost or personal social cost, experienced a deeper and more holistic level of healing.*46

By offering a holistic alternative to Patriarchy, Jesus offered more than just physical healing which might not be long-lasting. Jesus offered deep healing, a new way of life, and wholeness of spirit, mind, and body through the lifelong path of discipleship. This holistic path, by breaking away from Patriarchy and being molded and reshaped by following Jesus, is what restores "wholeness" and brings about a "new creation," a "new man," and a "new woman."

Such a big lifestyle change requires a strong commitment to taking a big step forward.

"As they were going along the road, someone said to him, 'I will follow you wherever you go.' And Jesus said to him, 'Foxes have holes, and birds of the air have nests; but the [Human One] has nowhere to lay his head.' To another he said, 'Follow me.' But he said, 'Lord, first let me go and bury my father.' But Jesus said to him, 'Let the dead bury their own dead; but as for you, go and proclaim the kingdom of God.' Another said, 'I will follow you, Lord; but let me first say farewell to those at my home.' Jesus said to him, 'No one who puts a hand to the plow and looks back is fit for the kingdom of God.'" (Luke 9:57-62) All who longingly look back at their lives in patriarchal society are looking in the wrong direction. They are not ready to follow Jesus and enter God's kingdom or commonwealth on Earth. They are not ready for Jesus' holistic path of working to overcome Patriarchy and being part of a New Creation on Earth.

Footnotes

1. Jeremy Rifkin with Ted Howard, Entropy: A New World View, Bantam Books, New York, 1980, p. 175.
2. Nukewatch Quarterly, Winter 2022-2023, citing Newsweek, October 10, 2022.
3. Erica L. Green, NY Times, "Amid Tragedy, Help Delivered," Star Tribune, February 5, 2023.
4. Allen G. Breed, AP, "How Tuskegee study was revealed to the nation," Star Tribune, July 31, 2022.
5. Jef Feeley, Bloomberg News, "Prison testing haunts J & J," Star Tribune, March 13, 2022.
6. Edward P. Ehlinger (physician & former commissioner of the Minnesota Department of Health), "Defund the health care system," Star Tribune, October 20, 2021.
7. Ivan Illich, Medical Nemesis, 1976, p. 17.
8. Zoya Teirstein, Grist, AP, "Climate change threatens health," Star Tribune, July 19, 2023.
9. Daniel Trotta, Reuters, "Cities drive climate change, UN says," Duluth News Tribune, April 5, 2022.
10. Charles Lee, "The Integrity of Justice," Sojourners, Feb. - Mar. 1990, p. 25.
11. Darryl Fears, Washington Post, "Redlining practice leaves a legacy of bad air quality," Star Tribune, March 10, 2022.
12. Edward P. Ehlinger.
13. Elisabeth Rosenthal, Kaiser Health News, "The debt crisis that sick Americans can't avoid," Star Tribune, August 8, 2022.
14. Rebecca Robbins, Katie Thomas, Jessica Silver-Greenberg, NY Times, "Hospitals helped pave their path to shortages," Star Tribune, December 25, 2022.

15. Janice Raymond, Women as Wombs, Harper San Francisco, 1993, pp. 14 & 91.
16. John F. Haught, Resting on the Future, Bloomsbury, 2015, pp. 159-160.
17. Juliet Macur, NY Times, "Nassar abuse survivors reach $380M settlement," Star Tribune, December 14, 2021.
18. Juliet Macur, Michael Levenson, NY Times, "FBI bungled probe of doctor, report says," Star Tribune, July 15, 2021.
19. News Services, "UCLA to pay $243M to settle abuse cases," Star Tribune, February 10, 2022.
20. News Services, "$165M settlement reached in sex abuse case," Star Tribune, October 9, 2022.
21. Janice Raymond, The Transsexual Empire: The Making of the She-Male, Columbia University, 1979, 1994, pp. 120 & 149.
22. Ivan Illich, p. 96.
23. Edward P. Ehlinger.
24. Lauran Neergaard, AP, "Speeding up sepsis care can save lives, study shows," Star Tribune, May 22, 2017.
25. Roni Caryn Rabin, NY Times, "Diagnostic device has critical flaw: cleanliness," Star Tribune, September 1, 2019.
26. Joe Carlson, "FDA halts sales of pelvic mesh," Star Tribune, April 17, 2019.
27. Joel Achenbach, Lenny Bernstein, Robert O'Harrow Jr., Shawn Boburg, Washington Post, "Epidemic Failure," Star Tribune, August 11, 2019.
28. Geoff Mulvihill, AP, "Opioid settlements clear way for $26 billion in aid," Star Tribune, February 27, 2022.
29. Jan Hoffman, NY Times, "Tribes reach $590M deal with J & J, others on opioids," Star Tribune, February 2, 2022.
30. Mike Stobbe, AP, "Overdose deaths set U.S. mark," Star Tribune, May 12, 2022.
31. Faye Flam, Bloomberg Opinion, "Antidepressant benefits were overpromised. So now what?," Star Tribune, August 10, 2022.
32. PA Media/dpa, "Drug Overdose," Duluth News Tribune, February 16, 2022.
33. W.J. Rorabaugh, Prohibition: A Concise History, Oxford University Press, New York, 2018, p. 2.
34. W.J. Rorabaugh, p. 9.
35. W.J. Rorabaugh, p. 38.
36. W.J. Rorabaugh, p. 44.
37. Aneri Pattani, Kaiser Health News, "Closing the gender gap in alcohol consumption," Star Tribune, July 4, 2021.

38. Gary Kohls, "Responding to a Radio Talk Show About Mental Illness, Duluth Reader, February 16, 2017.
39. Moriah Balingit, Washington Post, "More U.S. teens grappling with mental health issues, Star Tribune, April 1, 2022.
40. Kate Thayer, Chicago Tribune, "Has boozy mom culture gone too far?," Star Tribune, May 1, 2018.
41. Ericka Andersen, NY Times, "Women, do we need an intervention?," Star Tribune, April 5, 2022.
42. Jenna Ross, "Go Dry This Month," Star Tribune, January 2, 2022.
43. News Services, "Just one drink a day could shrink your brain," Star Tribune, March 27, 2022.
44. Erica Pearson, "Give it a rest," Star Tribune, January 9, 2022.
45. National Institute on Alcohol Abuse and Alcoholism, quoted by Rolf Fure in "A terrible link: 'Too much to drink' and sexual assault," Star Tribune, August 17, 2018.
46. For a more in-depth reading of this passage see Ched Myers, Binding The Strong Man: A Political Reading of Mark's Story of Jesus, Orbis Books, Maryknoll, New York, 1988.

Chapter 7

Patriarchy, Genocide, and Climate Chaos

The big-picture context for every problem, issue, or topic is a very broad understanding of Patriarchy. The basic premise of Patriarchy is male dominance and female subordination, resulting in hierarchy, inequality, oppression, and violence. Patriarchal societies standardize and institutionalize hierarchy, inequality, oppression, and violence.

Patriarchal civilizations are leading humanity down "the path of death and destruction." This can be hard to see when people are preoccupied with their personal problems and daily habits. A greater consciousness of the "big picture" is needed. Examining the topics of genocide and climate chaos can be helpful in seeing the big picture more clearly.

Genocide occurs when a dominant, powerful, and violent entity seeks to deliberately destroy, *in whole or in part*, a particular ethnic, racial, religious, cultural, or national group. The most extreme genocide involves massive violence to kill and exterminate a particular group. But "total genocide" is not the only form of genocide. The term "genocide" or "genocidal" may also apply to singular events—like dropping a nuclear bomb—or to a longer time period of killing, rape, land theft, human rights abuses, forced assimilation, and other policies designed to fragment, divide, break down, destroy, or diminish a particular group. An example of the latter form of genocide is the treatment of Native Americans by Canada and the United States over hundreds of years.

Genocide is a re-occurring phenomenon throughout patriarchal history. A genocide event is not an aberration of patriarchal civilization. It is not an isolated or unexpected event. It is not limited to a few monstrous male leaders and their henchmen. It is a chronic event that will continue to plague humanity throughout patriarchal history.

The roots of genocide are found in patriarchal civilizations. Patriarchal nation-states throughout the world are founded on dominative power, coercion, and violence. Every state supports hierarchy, inequality, oppression, and violence. Every state reserves for itself the right to use so-called "justified violence." States employ various police and military forces based on justified violence. This state-sponsored violence involves using "superior force," in order to govern and rule. Superior force is necessary for the state to maintain its rule and order. The concept of superior force means that "illegal" violence must, if deemed necessary by state authorities, be met with greater violence. So, the logic of so-called justified violence and superior force is built into the patriarchal state. They are the building blocks upon which the state may engage in war and genocide.

The roots of genocide run deeper in Patriarchy beyond just the government—and reach deeply into the general population. Patriarchy, through its hierarchical institutions, educational systems, doctrines, laws, myths, traditions, religions, and propaganda teaches so-called justified violence. Indoctrinated citizens and subjects and tribal members are led to believe in justified violence. Human violence against other humans is not innate—it is learned and chosen. The belief in justified violence finds a home in most people's hearts and minds. And from there, there are many possibilities and opportunities for violence to occur and grow.

There is a continuum of violence which represents different degrees of violence. The continuum of violence could be represented, moving from little violence to greater violence, as: spanking, slapping, punching, physical assault, rape, killing, mass murder, war, genocide. People who believe in and support justified violence can "slide" along the continuum of violence. Depending on different circumstances, perceived threats, self-interests, and proclaimed "national security threats" people can slide along the continuum and support greater and greater degrees of violence. Even individuals who might not engage in violent acts may be encouraged, pressured, or indoctrinated into supporting violent police forces, blindly supporting the troops, approving of killer drone missile attacks, and supporting war and its inevitable "collateral damage." Sliding along the continuum of violence towards greater violence is all too easy.

Most individuals are ready to slide along the continuum of violence towards greater violence whenever there is an escalation of trouble or "bad" violence. While individuals, as individuals, don't wage war or commit genocide, the "seeds" of war and genocide are within them.

Many individuals slide towards killing—and a very small number of individuals may even engage in a mass shooting, sometimes defined as four or more people killed. Mass shootings in the U.S. have become more common. Various explanations, none of which mention Patriarchy, have been presented as to the underlying causes for why individuals do them. The problem of mass shootings is exacerbated by mental health issues and not-so-effective drug treatments, homicidal and suicidal ideation, widespread availability of guns, social isolation, too much time online, violent video games, and a culture that glorifies ultra-violent superheroes.

Of course, the big-picture context is Patriarchy. Americans, that is American men, have a great love for guns, for gun culture, and for gun rights. 44% of U.S. households have at least one gun. Americans own over 400 million guns—mostly owned and wielded by men.

The widespread availability of guns inevitably leads to many men being killed by guns.

"About 60% of the gun deaths in the U.S. each year are suicides....Firearms accounted for about 8% of suicide attempts but slightly more than 50% of the 47,511 suicide deaths in 2019....White men are six times as likely to die by suicide as other Americans. Black men are 17 times as likely to be killed with a gun fired by someone else....Of the 90,498 gun deaths in 2020 and 2021, 38,796 were homicides. Nearly 21,000 of those victims were Black men." [*1] Mark Bergman, Lenny Bernstein, Dan Keating, Andrew Ba Tran, Artur Galocha

The vast majority of mass shootings are committed by men. They are deeply influenced by patriarchal culture.

"The motivations of men who commit mass shootings are often muddled, complex or unknown. But one common thread that connects many of them—other than access to powerful firearms—is a history of hating women, assaulting wives, girlfriends and female family members, or sharing misogynistic views online, researchers say....In more than half of all mass shootings in the United States from 2009 to 2017, an intimate partner or family member of the perpetrator was among the victims....In recent years, a number of these men have identified as so-called incels, short for involuntary celibates, an online subculture of men who express rage at women for denying them sex and who frequently fantasize about violence and celebrate mass shooters in their online discussion groups." *2 Julie Bosman, Kate Taylor, Tim Arango

Patriarchal culture "fragments the whole" and brings divisions among people. Mass murderers are largely socially disconnected, heartless, and lack all empathy for their victims.

The vast number of men in the U.S. with guns means that conflicts can easily escalate to shootings, to a spray of bullets, and to mass shootings. Besides those who are actually killed, there are many more who experience gunshot wounds which cause great long-term physical and psychological harm.

The greatest degrees of violence, i.e., war and genocide, are usually committed by armed forces (primarily men) but may have widespread support among the general population. Genocide represents an extreme form of violence—but it is not a big step beyond war. Genocide may just be a further extension of war—and some war events may be viewed accurately as genocidal. Many wars offer a possibility for armed forces to "slide" into genocide. There are numerous examples of genocide throughout patriarchal history.

As mentioned above, the United States (as well as Canada) over a long period of time had conflicts and policies which, when looked at collectively, amounted to genocide against Native Americans. The United States used numerous policies toward the Native Americans to divide and conquer them. A major goal of U.S. policies was "land acquisition," i.e., land theft. The U.S. used its superior military power to fight battles, commit massacres, pressure tribes into less-than-fair treaties, and defend U.S. violation of the treaties—in order to continue gaining more Native land. At times Native Americans were hunted down and killed and bounty payments were given for Native scalps. The Indian Removal Act in 1830 was an example of "ethnic cleansing," forcing some Native American tribes to abandon their homelands and move far westward. Policies and practices were used to break down tribes' economic way of life, destroy the Native food system, and destroy Native cultures. The slaughter, nearly to extinction, of tens of millions of buffalo by white men in the 19th century impoverished many Native American tribes' food system. In 1887, Congress passed the General Allotment Act or the Dawes Act. The law helped to break down communal Native landownership traditions and facilitated another land grab of Native lands. White men's "gifts" to Native Americans also included diseases, alcohol, pollution, and radiation.

An often neglected part of the white-settler oppression of Native Americans was Indian slavery. Indian slavery was widespread throughout the Americas but white North Americans significantly contributed to it, particularly in the West and Southwest.

"Native Americans had enslaved each other for millennia, but with the arrival of Europeans, practices of captivity originally embedded in specific cultural contexts became commodified, expanded in unexpected ways, and came to resemble the kinds of human trafficking that are recognizable to us today....If we were to add up all the Indian slaves taken in the New World from the time of Columbus to the end of the nineteenth century, the figure would run somewhere between 2.5 and 5 million slaves....
[I]n stark contrast to the African slave trade, which consisted primarily of adult males, the majority of Indian slaves were actually women and children....Sexual exploitation and women's reproductive capabilities are part of the answer....
By buying Indian children, the Mormons would be giving impetus to a terrible traffic that caused bloodshed, mayhem, and war. Therefore Brigham Young's solution was to steer a middle and contradictory course: he cracked down on some traffickers but also advocated the passage of the Act for the Relief of Indian Slaves and Prisoners of 1852, which enabled Utah residents to become guardians of Indian minors for up to twenty years." *3 Andres Resendez

Another practice that helped to contribute to an overall practice of genocide was the taking of Native children by white Americans. Beginning in 1879 the U.S. government began forcibly taking Native American children to off-reservation so-called "boarding schools."

> "Captain Richard H. Pratt's boarding school experiment began in the late nineteenth century....he offered a variation of the slogan—popular in the American West—that stated the only good Indian was a dead one. The proper goal, Pratt claimed, was to 'kill the Indian...and save the man.' Pratt founded a school in 1879 at the site of an unused cavalry barracks at Carlisle, Pennsylvania, organizing the institution along rigid military lines." *4 MN Historical Society

Many more white-supremacist boarding schools were formed. While government-run schools predominated, many churches became involved in managing schools.

> "U.S. religious groups were affiliated [with] at least 156 such schools, according to the National Native American Boarding School Healing Coalition....That's more than 40% of the 367 schools documented so far by the coalition." *5 Peter Smith

The Coalition has now identified 523 schools in 38 states.

Forcibly placing Native children in white-supremacist boarding schools was a form of state-sponsored kidnapping, child slavery, and institutionalized child abuse.

> "At these boarding schools, administrators, teachers, disciplinarians, and others worked to destroy Indian languages, religions, and ways of life. The government used the boarding schools as a means of physically separating children from their parents, grandparents, and communities and sought to use the school experience to supplant traditional Native values and culture with those of the dominant American society." *6 Brenda J. Child

Child abuses were widespread and severe—with beatings, sexual abuse, and many children dying.

> "Boarding school remains a burning historical memory for Indians. Like the Trail of Tears or Wounded Knee, boarding school is symbolic of American colonialism at its most genocidal." *7 Brenda J. Child

The totality of U.S. policies against Native Americans amounted to genocide and has left a devastating legacy of continuing oppression, exploitation, and impoverishment of Native Americans.

> "Native children continued to be removed from their homes at staggering rates through adoption." *8 Jessica Washington

To this day Native families continue to be broken apart.

A racist patriarchal society places a lower value on women and people of color. Native women, in particular, continue to be targeted for violence and sexual abuse. When Native women are abducted or murdered the mainstream media and public do not give it the same attention given to white women who are abducted or murdered. Consequently, there is an
> "epidemic of violence against Native American women and girls, who face staggeringly high rates of sexual assault and violence....The National Institute of Justice found in 2016 that more than half of all Native American women have experienced sexual violence in their lifetimes — and 97% of those women were victimized by a non-Native offender....Native women are also more likely to be targeted by sex traffickers....'It made reservations perfect hunting grounds for predators,' said Lisa Brunner, a citizen of the White Earth Band of Ojibwe....[Marisa Miakonda] Cummings said sexual violence against Native women from nontribal members has been happening since the first settlers arrived. The trauma is generational and passed down from mothers to daughters." *9 Briana Bierschbach

In a patriarchal society the vast majority of predators are men. And it is male predators who are primarily the driving force of the "epidemic of violence against Native American women and girls."

The 20th century saw many examples of patriarchal civilizations engaging in war and genocide. The Ottoman Turks genocide against Armenians began in 1915. An estimated 1.5 million Armenians "were deported, massacred or marched to their deaths in a campaign of extermination by Ottoman Empire forces." *10 Millions were victimized under Josef Stalin's rule in Russia and the Ukraine.
> "In the early 1930s, a mass, man-made famine resulted in the Holodomor, which essentially means genocide by starvation, according to Ellen J. Kennedy....The collectivization of agriculture and a perceived need to extinguish any yearning of Ukrainian independence, let alone identity, led to the deaths of about 3.5 million (the world will never know the true toll of Josef Stalin's homicidal rule in Ukraine and elsewhere in the Soviet Union). At the height of the Holodomor, Kennedy said, Ukrainians were reportedly dying at a rate of 28,000 a

day...and an estimated 30% of those starved were children under the age of 10." *11 John Rash

The most infamous case of genocide, called the Holocaust, was committed by Nazi Germany during World War II. Six million European Jews, in particular, were systematically exterminated in Nazi concentration camps. This large-scale and well-organized mass slaughter epitomizes how economically and educationally "advanced" patriarchal civilizations can slide into full-blown genocide.

During World War II, as during wars in general, there were always pressures to escalate the fighting and to slide towards using greater violence. The pressures are always strong because once war has begun, neither side wants to be on the losing side of war. World War II was the "cauldron" for the development of nuclear weapons—the most powerful and destructive weapons ever built. They are genocidal weapons of mass destruction. They have been used only twice—both times by the United States—on the civilian populations of Hiroshima and Nagasaki, Japan, near the end of World War II in 1945. The effects of the two bombs were horrendous, initially killing over 200,000 people. But, not to be overlooked, there were also massive and indiscriminate firebombings of civilian cities during World War II which resulted in the deaths of more civilians than was caused by the two atomic bombs. War and genocide are escalations of violence. They often coincide—as patriarchal political and military leaders seek to accomplish their objectives by any means necessary.

Another notable 20th century example of war and genocide occurred in Southeast Asia in the 1960s. The United States committed genocidal bombings that killed and injured millions of civilians in Vietnam, Cambodia, and Laos.

In general, wars are fought primarily by men in the military—and yet wars result in large numbers of civilian casualties. Which unarmed civilians account for most of those unfairly victimized by wars?

"In our contemporary world, according to Amnesty International, 90 per cent of casualties in modern warfare are civilian and of these 75 per cent are women and children....'Women and girls are uniquely and disproportionately affected by armed conflict. Women bear the brunt of war and are the vast majority of casualties resulting from war. Women are 80% of all refugees and displaced persons. Rape and sexual violence targeting women and girls are routinely used not only to terrorize women, but as strategic tools of war and instruments of genocide.'" *12

Victimized women and girls in wartime are terrorized and traumatized by rape, gang rape, sexual slavery, torture, and physical injuries—and then, in so-called "peacetime" many experience social rejection from patriarchal families and communities and suffer lifelong economic hardships.

So, a particularly patriarchal and genocidal feature of many wars is the mass rape of women and girls. This patriarchal feature has occurred throughout the ages. Women and girls are often targeted by men in invading military forces. This deliberate policy can help to decimate an "enemy group" by destroying the family, community, and ethnic or national cohesiveness of the victimized group. This policy is not a relic of the distant past. Like war and genocide, it continues to happen over and over again.

"In the 100 days of genocide that ravaged the small African nation of Rwanda, an estimated 250,000 to 500,000 women and girls were raped. In Sierra Leone, between 1991 and 2000, about 64,000 internally displaced women endured sexual assault. In the Balkans tensions of the 1990s, thousands of women in Bosnia-Herzegovina and Kosovo experienced terrible violations involving mass rape: 20,000 to 50,000 women were violated in the Bosnian conflict over three years. During the Liberian civil war, from 1999 to 2003, about 49 per cent of women aged 15 to 70 experienced sexual violence from soldiers or armed militia. In the early 2000s Janjaweed paramilitary and Sudanese government troops raped and murdered tens of thousands of non-Arab women in Darfur. In the Democratic Republic of the Congo, an estimated 200,000 surviving rape victims are alive today, although the figure for those who were killed will probably never be known. At least 50,000 babies were born through the rape of their mothers." *13 Elaine Storkey

Mass rape is a thoroughly patriarchal tactic where men with military training and weapons are given license to use great violence against women and girls with impunity.

Male soldiers who engage in mass rape of women and girls may experience a form of misogynistic male bonding. In general, patriarchal masculinity values male dominance, aggressiveness, sexual virility, and violence against "enemies." During war, during intensive life-or-death situations, male soldiers can bond in male comradeship during collective efforts for survival and attacks against "enemies." Violent attacks against females who are part of an "enemy group" can contribute to patriarchal male-soldier-bonding. Mass rape of women and girls by male soldiers doesn't require that the soldiers experience strong feelings of hatred for their specific female victims (although some may). More important is the objectification of the victims, male-peer expectations, and the freedom to unleash violent attacks against the female targets.

Of course, on a deep level mass rape of females involves deep-rooted misogyny. It involves a deep-level hatred of female being and a trained and internalized aggression of skilled military fighters—who are a force that is essentially anti-life. On the continuum of violence mass rape of females fits well with war and genocide (and gynocide). Male wartime atrocities, which keep reoccurring, may symbolize Patriarchy's historical and global "war against life-giving female being."

> "These acts of violation/violence are expressions of the War State's essential identity as the State of Rapism, in which all invasions, occupations, destructions of 'enemy territory' are elaborations upon the theme of rape/gynocide." *14 Mary Daly

Patriarchy continues to rule through war, genocide, and mass rapes in the 21st century. The very patriarchal Islamic State in Iraq and the Levant (ISIL or ISIS) were waging war to expand their territory or caliphate. Their attack on the Yazidi religious minority group in Iraq, both increased the territory under their rule and provided a supply of women and girls for their male fighters.

> "ISIL's formal introduction of systematic sexual slavery dates to Aug. 3, 2014, when its fighters invaded the villages on the southern flank of Mount Sinjar in northern Iraq. It's valleys and ravines are home to the Yazidis, a religious minority….In village after village, the men and older boys were driven or marched to nearby fields, where they were forced to lie down in the dirt and sprayed with automatic fire. The women, girls and children, however, were hauled off in open-bed trucks….Then, inevitably,

they were sent in smaller groups to Syria or to elsewhere in Iraq, where they were bought and sold for sex....In much the same way as specific Bible passages were used to support the U.S. slave trade, ISIL cites specific verses or stories in Quran or else in the Sunna, the traditions based on the sayings and deeds of the prophet Mohammed, to justify their human trafficking....Cole Bunzel, a scholar of Islamic theology at Princeton University....points to the corpus of Islamic jurisprudence, which he says includes detailed rules for the treatment of slaves....'You can argue that it is no longer relevant and has fallen into abeyance. [ISIL] would argue that these institutions need to be revived, because that is what the Prophet and his companions did.'" *15 Rukmini Callimachi

The use of patriarchal religious and ideological rationales for the sexual exploitation of women, girls, and slaves still exists today.

The patriarchal military leaders of Myanmar/Burma recently engaged in a case of ethnic cleansing peaking in August 2017. But the persecution of the minority has a longer history.

"The Rohingya Muslim ethnic minority from Myanmar's western Rakhine state has faced systematic persecution at the hands of the Buddhist majority for decades. The military junta that ruled the nation for decades stripped them of their citizenship....For a people who have already lived through unimaginable horrors, including mass rapes and brutal killings...it seems as if the misery will never end." *16 Muneeza Naqvi

In a patriarchal world, minorities in every nation are vulnerable at various times to very intense persecution by more powerful majorities. And women and girls are like "pawns," like "soft targets," for patriarchal power moves.

"The rape of Rohingya women by Myanmar's security forces has been sweeping and methodical, the Associated Press found in interviews with 29 women and girls....The testimonies bolster the U.N.'s contention that Myanmar's armed forces are systematically employing rape as a 'calculated tool of terror' aimed at exterminating the Rohingya people." *17 Kristen Gelineau

The atrocities are very intentional, planned, and directed and amount to genocide.

"[T]he United States...formally accused Myanmar of committing genocide against its minority Rohingya

> population….Canada, France, Turkey and other U.S. allies have already declared the 2017 rampage to be genocide….'The evidence also points to a clear intent behind these mass atrocities—the intent to destroy Rohingya,' [Antony] Blinken said." *18 Lara Jakes

Another recent example of conflict escalating into war, mass rapes, and genocide began in November 2020 when Ethiopian forces attacked the northern Ethiopian Tigrayan ethnic group.

> "To date, researchers estimate that up to 500,000 Ethiopians have died from war and famine in the 17 months since Ethiopian Prime Minister Abiy Ahmed and his partner in war, Eritrean dictator Isaias Afwerki, plotted to turn a political conflict with the TPLF [Tigray People's Liberation Front] into a genocidal military conflict." *19 Steve Andreasen

The patriarchal male leaders and military forces escalated the conflict to targeting and punishing an entire civilian population. Of course, atrocities abounded.

> "More than 1,200 cases of sexual violence were documented by health centers in Tigray between February and April alone, Amnesty [International] said. No one knows the real toll…as most of the health facilities across the region of 6 million people were looted or destroyed. These numbers are likely a 'small fraction' of the reality, Amnesty said." *20 Cara Anna

Mass rapes of Tigrayan women and girls by military men was only one part of the violence and terror unleashed against the civilian population. Mass rapes have been accompanied with massacres, ethnic cleansing and mass expulsions, torture, arbitrary detentions, destruction of health facilities, livestock pillaging, cutting off banking and telecommunication services, blocking humanitarian aid and fuel supplies to the region, and creating a man-made hunger and malnutrition crisis.

> "Half of pregnant or lactating women in Tigray are malnourished, as well as a third of children under 5, leading to stunting and maternal death, the [World Food Program] report found." *21 Giulia Paravicini

Punishing innocent mothers and children is just part of all-out patriarchal war strategies. It's part of across-the-board collective punishment of the designated "enemy population."

There are so many recent examples of genocide. China continues to target the Uyghur ethnic minority with severe persecution and abuses. The Saudi-led attacks, with U.S. military weapons, against the Houthis in Yemen has created a huge humanitarian crisis. Russia's brutal invasion of the Ukraine, with serious risks of ever-more escalating violence, has had devastating effects on the civilian population. Israel's total naval blockade of the Gaza Strip, massive bombing campaign of civilian structures, massive displacement of the civilian population, and military land invasion of Gaza appears to be a textbook case of genocide.

One point of looking at these examples of genocide is to emphasize that genocide is a re-occurring event throughout patriarchal history. Genocide is not an aberration of patriarchal civilization. It is a common (on a world field) outcome of patriarchal civilization. Genocide is not just a terrible event of the past. It is either a present reality somewhere in the world or a threat to happen at any time. Another important point is that "Patriarchy" needs to be named in order to "connect the dots"— to reveal the connections throughout time and various locations. Ultimately it is "Patriarchy" that needs to be overcome.

Climate Change/Chaos

Although climate change/chaos is a global event, developing over hundreds of years during the fossil fuel era, it has some intersections with genocide, and is attributable to how patriarchal civilizations have regarded nature and exploited the Earth's resources. To say that climate change/chaos is caused and driven by "human activities and human pollution" conceals much. Patriarchal civilizations have developed an exploitive capitalistic economic system. Capitalism creates labor hierarchies which have unequal power and unequal rewards. Stockholders/owners and management have the most power and reap the most benefits. Capitalism funnels most of the wealth created to those at the top of the economic hierarchies. The earth's resources and lower-level labor are exploited in order to maximize profits and wealth. In the fossil-fuel era, patriarchal capitalism's expansion has released enormous greenhouse gas emissions (heating up the planet), created tremendous amounts of pollution (despoiling the environment), overexploited natural resources (undermining ecosystems), and resulted in great inequalities of wealth and poverty. Thus climate change/chaos is not caused simply by the euphemism "human activities," but is more accurately described as being *caused and driven by global patriarchal capitalism.*

It has been stated that the world is in "advanced ecological overshoot." This means that natural resources are being overexploited, which is not sustainable in the long run and is harmful to ecosystems in the present time. But this "ecological overshoot" should not be attributed simply to "human activities" or to humanity in general. It is due to patriarchal capitalism, the rich and powerful, and to large corporations. The "carbon footprint" of the rich and powerful dwarfs that of all the people living in poverty.

> "The consumption habits of the wealthiest 10% of people generate three times more pollution than those of the poorest 50%, the [United Nations Intergovernmental Panel on Climate Change] report said....The suffering is worst in the world's poorest countries and low-lying island nations, which are home to roughly 1 billion people yet account for less than 1% of humanity's total planet-warming pollution, the report says." *22 Sarah Kaplan

Powerful men bear the most responsibility for the climate change/chaos crisis, although all affluent people share some complicity in the crisis.

Closely related to patriarchal capitalism as a significant driver of climate change/chaos is patriarchal militarism. The gigantic United States military, which dwarves all other nations in military spending and energy consumption, is "the single largest institutional emitter of greenhouse gases." Military forces consume enormous amounts of fossil fuels and are not held accountable for their extravagant use.

Also closely related to the climate change/chaos crisis is the extinction crisis. We are currently living during what appears to be Earth's 6th great age of mass extinctions of species. It may not be as dramatic as the first five ages of mass extinctions. It may be necessary to tune in to what scientists are reporting, to move away from highly-developed patriarchal civilization, and to integrate more into the natural world. Even as the human population continues to grow—perhaps indicating the world's crises are not so bad—this growth is not sustainable in a patriarchal world. The human population is related to and connected with the populations of other species and the health of the environment. The extinction crisis engulfs us all. It's not only a matter of how many species will go extinct this century. It is also a matter of the extraordinary drop in numbers of the populations of those species that may survive—and the growing harm to ecosystems. Everything is connected. A massive decline of biodiversity and the breakdown of ecosystems means that most species in the world are under serious threat.

> "Have humans [patriarchal capitalism] damaged the Earth's ecosystems so severely that we're well on our way to the biggest mass extinction since the dinosaurs vanished 66 million years ago?....A study published... paints a grim picture....The authors describe the shrinking population of species as 'a massive erosion of the greatest biological diversity in the history of Earth.' 'Thus, we emphasize that the sixth mass extinction is already here and the window for effective action is very short, probably two or three decades at most,' the authors wrote....The driving force is a steady drumbeat of human [patriarchal and capitalist] activities that result in habitat losses, pollution and climate disruption, among others. 'The massive loss of populations and species reflects our lack of empathy to all the wild species that have been our companions since our origins,' the study's lead author, Gerardo Ceballos, an ecology professor at the Universidad Nacional Autonoma de Mexico in Mexico, said." *23 Kristine Phillips

Our "lack of empathy" for other species can be attributed to Patriarchy which "fragments the whole," leads to greater separation of humans from nature, and creates an oppressive, anthropocentric, and exploitive society.

> Small species are very important to every ecosystem. "The global extinction crisis underway may be more intense than previously thought as humans [patriarchal civilizations] continue to tear up land, overuse certain resources and heat up the planet, new research led by the University of Minnesota indicates. Nearly 1 in 3 species of all kinds—30%—face global extinction or have been driven to extinction since the year 1500....That's significantly higher than prevailing global estimates and the findings surprised lead author Forest Isbell....He said one of the reasons is that it takes more insects and other lesser-studied species groups into account....'The majority of species on the planet are plants and insects

> and other invertebrate animals that we know so little about'....[Healy Hamilton] said, 'And yet those are the very species which help purify our air, filter our water, maintain the health of our soils, pollinate plants we need for food, fuel, and fiber, and provide medicines to hundreds of millions of people.'" *24 Jennifer Bjorhus

Despite the alienating construction of patriarchal civilization, human beings are still a part of nature, are still connected to other species in various ecosystems, and are still in a relationship of interdependency with other species.

Patriarchal capitalism and militarism are steadily weakening ecosystems, the foundations of biodiversity and life.

> "Humans [patriarchal capitalism and militarism] have been simplifying nature and thinning it out—creating a world that is far less stable and resilient, [David] Tilman said....Tilman, the University of Minnesota ecologist, estimates the world is losing species at a rate roughly 100 times what it was in the past. That's based largely on data about birds and mammals, he said, which are the most studied." *25 Jennifer Bjorhus

As ecosystems destabilize and biodiversity declines, human life becomes more precarious. As climate chaos worsens more places will become unlivable. The number of economic and environmental refugees will skyrocket. No nation will be untouched by massive human migration.

Recognizing the high rate of extinctions is important—as is recognizing *how fast things are changing*. The speed of change can affect species' ability to adapt and survive. A great age of mass extinctions overcomes most species' ability to adapt.

> "New research suggests the accelerating fires of this apocalyptic period 252 million years ago were not just a symptom of a warming planet, but a driver of extinction in their own right....These events took place in an event known as the End-Permian Extinction, or the Great Dying....By the time it was over, most living things on Earth—up to 95% of ocean species, and more than 70% of those on land—were dead....The new study highlights eerie parallels between that ancient period of global warming and our own. 'There's a sort of interplay between the present and the past,' said Chris Mays, a paleontologist at University College Cork in Ireland and

lead author of the study....'We're warming up the world on the scale of hundreds of years, and there's a good chance that when you increase temperatures and change the environment at such a rapid pace, that's when ecosystems break down,' Mays said. 'The pace of change is actually really important'....The human-caused [Patriarchy-caused] warming Earth faces in the foreseeable future isn't yet as extreme as the temperature swings of the Permian period, but it is [happening] faster. 'Nature ran the experiment already,' [David] Bottjer said. 'It's not a pretty sight.'" *26 Corinne Purtill

Human beings, due to the fossil-fuel infrastructure and institutions of patriarchal civilizations, are slow to adapt to the worsening conditions of climate change/chaos.
"Earth is in more hot water than ever before, and so are we, an expert United Nations climate panel warned in a grim new report....Sea levels are rising at an ever-faster rate as ice and snow shrink, and oceans are getting more acidic and losing oxygen, the Inter-governmental Panel on Climate Change said....'The oceans and the icy parts of the world are in big trouble, and that means we're all in big trouble, too,' said one of the report's lead authors, Michael Oppenheimer, professor of geo-sciences and international affairs at Princeton University. 'The changes are accelerating'....The oceans absorb more than 90% of the excess heat from carbon pollution in the air, as well as much of the carbon dioxide itself....'Climate change is already irreversible,' French climate scientist Valerie Masson-Delmotte, a report lead author said....'Due to the heat uptake in the ocean, we can't go back.'" *27 Seth Borenstein
Patriarchy is driving the rapidly-developing climate crisis—and the response of humanity needs to be extraordinary.

Large forests, like the Amazon rainforest, have been referred to as "carbon sinks," absorbing large amounts of carbon dioxide, and also referred to as "the lungs of the planet," for their contribution of oxygen to the planet. But a combination of patriarchal development and global warming is putting extra stress on forests. The Amazon rainforest is getting hit hard.
"Yet satellite images taken over the past several decades reveal that more than 75% of the rain forest is losing resilience, according to a study....The vegetation is drier

and takes longer to regenerate after a disturbance. Even the most densely forested tracks struggle to bounce back. This widespread weakness offers an early warning sign that the Amazon is nearing its 'tipping point,' the study's authors say. Amid rising temperatures and other human [patriarchal] pressures, the ecosystem could suffer sudden and irreversible dieback. More than half of the rain forest could be converted into savanna in a matter of decades."
*28 Sarah Kaplan

Not heeding the warnings could result in cataclysmic environmental consequences. But patriarchal deforestation seems to continue on a "business-as-usual" basis.

"The annual report by the World Resources Institute… found that tropical regions lost 9.3 million acres of primary old-growth forest in 2021. That resulted in 2.5 billion metric tons of emissions of carbon dioxide, or about 2 1/2 times as much as emitted by passenger cars and light trucks in the United States each year….Rod Taylor, global director of the institute's global forests program, said that the essentially flat rate of deforestation over the past four years was not good 'for the climate, for the extinction crisis, and for the fate of many forest peoples.' Most forest loss in the tropics is linked to agriculture or other activities, like mining. Forests are clear cut and often burned, and these fires can grow out of control, adding to the devastation….A recent study showed that the Amazon, the world's largest tropical forestlands, is less able to recover from disturbances like drought and logging, and that at least part of the region is approaching a threshold where it will shift from forest to grasslands. 'That would release enough carbon into the atmosphere to blow the Paris Agreement goals right out of the water,' [Frances] Seymour said. 'No one should even think anymore about planting trees instead of reducing emissions from fossil fuels,' she said. 'It's got to be both, and it's got to be now before it's too late.'" *29 Henry Fountain

The Amazon rainforest is just one of many parts of the world that are moving towards disastrous "tipping points." Unfortunately, patriarchal civilizations, with all their infrastructure and global economic ties, have built-in inertia. A "business-as-usual" approach to climate change/chaos not only means that "the worst is yet to come," since that is certain no matter what, but it also means that "the worst" will be really, really bad.

Clearing rainforests for more land for animal production and meat production is the number one contributor to deforestation. It is a double whammy for the environment with the carbon absorption of forests being replaced with major carbon releases through animal and meat production. Animal production contributes to very inefficient use of grains, water, and energy per calorie of food produced for human consumption. It exacerbates shortages of affordable grains and drinkable water for poor people. Animal production contributes to land, water, and air pollution and ecosystem degradation. Unless there is a significant reduction of global meat consumption, humanity's efforts to mitigate the worsening effects of climate change/chaos will be stymied.

It should also be noted that animal factory farms contribute to the distress, cruelty, and suffering of animals. Human liberation is connected to "animal liberation." Any separation of human liberation from nature means upholding patriarchal fragmentation.

Despite a steady roll-out of alarming scientific reports on climate change/chaos, patriarchal capitalism continues its exploitation of fossil fuels.

> "An emerging domain of research shows that plastic consumption and pollution harms human health—particularly for the world's poor....'Plastic threatens human health at every stage of its production pipeline—from the extraction of the fossil carbon, oil and gas, that is plastic's main constituent, to its manufacture, use and disposal,' said Philip Landrigan, director of the Global Observatory on Pollution and Health....Plastics use the same amount of oil as the entire aviation industry—and are expected to more than triple in their oil consumption in the next 30 years. Moreover, the pollution caused by petrochemical plants—which are most often in lower-income areas—threaten the health of communities. 'Plastic manufacture is inequitably distributed, with virtually all plastic production facilities located either in low- and mid-income countries or in poor and minority communities within high-income countries,' Landrigan said." *30 Erika Veidis & Jamie Hansen

Plastic production is expected to grow significantly in the coming decades. This will result in greater harm to the environment and to poor people and minorities in particular.

Climate change/chaos is going to have a big impact on patriarchal agricultural systems. Patriarchal agriculture features: large fields of mono-crops, high inputs of energy, fertilizers, and pesticides, much irrigation and exploitation of aquifers and rivers, use of large machinery, reliance on migrants and other so-called "cheap labor," as well as very large animal "factory farms" (with pigs, turkeys, chickens, etc.). A huge amount of food is currently being produced but climate change/chaos will put tremendous stress on this system.

> "Climatic models show a decline in global crop yields every decade going forward as the pressures of global warming intensify, punishing food producers with drought, heat, flooding, superstorms, invasive insects, shifting seasons and bacterial blights....By midcentury, the world may reach a threshold of global warming 'beyond which current agricultural practices can no longer support large human civilizations,' the International Panel on Climate Change has warned. U.S. Department of Agriculture scientist Jerry Hatfield put it to me this way: 'The single biggest threat of climate change is the collapse of food systems.'" *31 Amanda Little

The planet is on the path to ever-rising temperatures, which will be harder to cope with.

> "Failure to act now won't only condemn humanity to a hotter planet, the IPCC says. It will also make it impossible for future generations to cope with their changed environment. Beyond 1.5 degrees [Celsius] of warming, the IPCC says, humanity will run up against 'hard limits' to adaptation. Temperatures will get too high to grow many staple crops. Droughts will become so severe that even the strongest water conservation measures can't compensate." *32 Sarah Kaplan

Patriarchal history has instances of the collapse of civilizations and empires when their food system collapses. How quickly humans can adapt and change to a more sustainable and decentralized food production system is only a small part of the problem. Patriarchal capitalism and militarism and climate chaos, on a global scale, have to be addressed. By necessity human lifestyles will change, either willingly or unwillingly.

Water, in its various forms and locations, is undergoing significant changes which will adversely impact just about everything, including agriculture and food production.

"Many of the aquifers that supply 90% of the nation's water systems, and which have transformed vast stretches of America into some of the world's most bountiful farmland, are being severely depleted. These declines are threatening irreversible harm to the U.S, economy and society as a whole. The New York Times conducted one of the most comprehensive examinations of groundwater depletion nationwide and found that America's life-giving resource is being exhausted in much of the country, and in many cases it won't come back. Huge industrial farms and sprawling cities are draining aquifers that could take centuries or millenniums to replenish themselves, if they recover at all. States and communities are already paying the price." *33 Mira Rojanasakul, Christopher Flavelle, Blacki Migliozzi, Eli Murray

The increasing level of water vapor in the atmosphere will have harmful effects both on agricultural production and on urban living. In a "feedback loop," rising temperatures increase water vapor which then increases temperatures. Increases in heat and humidity adversely affect outdoor labor, food production, and all the poor people who lack air conditioning. Most cities suffer from an urban "heat island" effect, where urban areas retain more heat than outlying areas.

"[A]s many of South Asia's already scorching cities get even hotter, scientists and economists are warning of a quieter, more far-reaching danger: Extreme heat is devastating the health and livelihoods of tens of millions more. If global greenhouse gas emissions continue at their current pace, they say, heat and humidity levels could become unbearable, especially for the poor. It is already making them poorer and sicker....'These cities are going to become unlivable unless urban governments put in systems of dealing with this phenomenon,'...said Sujata Saunik." *34 Somini Sengupta

June through December 2023 set new monthly records for the warmest months ever recorded. 2023 set a new world record for the hottest year ever at 1.48 degrees Celsius above preindustrial times. Of course the heat is also pushing up ocean temperatures.

"The world's oceans—more than 70% of the Earth's surface—were the hottest ever recorded, nearly 69.8 F, and have set high temperature marks for three consecutive months, the WMO [World Meteorological Organization] and Copernicus [the European climate service] said….Climatologist Andrew Weaver said the WMO and Copernicus numbers come as no surprise, bemoaning how governments have not appeared to take the issue of global warming seriously enough. 'It's time for global leaders to start telling the truth,' said Weaver, a professor at the School of Earth and Ocean Sciences at the University of Victoria in British Columbia. 'We will not limit warming to 1.5 C; we will not limit warming to 2.0 C. It's all hands on deck now to prevent 3.0 C global warming —a level of warming that will wreak havoc worldwide.'"
*35 Jamey Keaton, Seth Borenstein

While devastating floods are becoming more common, there is also a growing scarcity of drinkable fresh water in most areas of the world.

"Many of the water systems that keep ecosystems thriving and feed a growing human population have become stressed. Rivers, lakes, and aquifers are drying up or becoming too polluted to use. More than half the world's wetlands have disappeared….Water scarcity…is what will wreak havoc….growing shortages of fresh water, rather than land, will become the Achilles' heel of global agricultural development….the Middle East…holds less than 1 percent of the world's fresh water….the groundwater reserves in India are among the lowest in the world….As a direct result of this severe, ongoing drop in water tables in northern (and western) China, deserts are now expanding at a rate of 1,400 square miles a year….Nearly 20 percent of China is desert….Water is now China's Achilles' heel….because of its scarcity, and because of its pollution." *36 Jeff Nesbit

Only about 2% of the water on Earth is fresh water—and some of that is melting and flowing into the oceans. Ice melt from Greenland is releasing large amounts of fresh water into the ocean.

"Melt rates have been increasing in the past two decades, and Greenland is the largest single ice-based contributor to the rate of global sea-level rise, surpassing contributions from both the larger Antarctic ice sheet and from mountain glaciers around the world....3.3% of Greenland's total ice volume will melt no matter what happens....One of the study authors said that more than 120 trillion tons of ice is already doomed to melt from the warming ice sheet's inability to replenish its edges. When that ice melts into water, if it were concentrated only over the United States, it would be 37 feet deep." *37 Seth Borenstein

Of course, in a warming planet, melt rates will continue to increase, and more of Greenland's ice sheet will melt. New developments are occurring in Antarctica.

"An ice shelf the size of New York City has collapsed in East Antarctica, an area long thought to be stable....It happened at the beginning of a freakish warm spell... when temperatures soared more than 70 degrees warmer than normal in some spots of East Antarctica....The issue isn't the amount of ice lost in this collapse, [Peter] Neff and [Catherine] Walker said. That is negligible. It's more about where it happened. Neff said he worries that previous assumptions about East Antarctica's stability may not be correct. And that's important because if the water frozen in East Antarctica melted - and that's a millennia-long process if not longer - it would raise seas across the globe more than 160 feet." *38 Seth Borenstein

There are many more topics related to climate change/chaos that could be described. The topics that have been discussed briefly here are meant to show that the crisis is real, deep, happening now, *brought about by patriarchal capitalism and militarism*, and will have long-term devastating effects no matter what changes are made. Even in the midst of such a crisis it can be hard to maintain a day-to-day consciousness of the gravity of the crisis. This is, in part, due to living in the mind-numbing consumerist, materialistic, and urban cultures of patriarchal civilizations. In order to get to the roots of Earth's crises it is essential to name "Patriarchy" and to seek ways to overcome Patriarchy.

So, do people really believe that governments and large corporations will provide effective leadership in addressing climate chaos and finding effective ways to mitigate its worsening effects? There are many global conferences on climate change/chaos with top political leaders in attendance. There are many speeches, promises, and resolutions. But, how much of it is just national and corporate "greenwashing" and more "blah, blah, blah"? Do the world's leaders address Patriarchy or patriarchal capitalism and militarism? Climate chaos will undoubtedly continue to worsen. In the long run any "solution" to climate chaos will need to address overcoming Patriarchy.

<u>Jesus and the Discipleship/Liberation Movement</u>

As stated before, the only true hope for overcoming Patriarchy is through Jesus and his discipleship/liberation movement. Jesus calls people to "come out" of Patriarchy and to follow him and to become part of a discipleship/liberation movement that is completely against the continuing rule of Patriarchy. Jesus' discipleship/liberation movement is meant to be a holistic and powerful (Spirit-power) alternative to Patriarchy.

Whatever people's circumstances are in a patriarchal society, Jesus continually offers people a new life if they choose to follow Jesus. Jesus' offer applies to all people, to both victims and perpetrators alike. Jesus offers new life through the path of discipleship, personal transformation, and opposition to Patriarchy.

Jesus calls people to a new way of life based on love and nonviolence, egalitarianism, service to others, prayer and worship, etc. Jesus teaches nonviolence and love for all people, including enemies. Jesus teaches:
> "You have heard that it was said, 'You shall love your neighbor and hate your enemy.' But I say to you, Love your enemies and pray for those who persecute you, so that you may be children of your Father [/ Mother] in heaven; for [God] makes [the] sun rise on the evil and on the good, and sends rain on the righteous and on the unrighteous. For if you love those who love you, what reward do you have? Do not even the tax collectors do the same?....Be perfect, therefore, as your Heavenly Father [/ Mother] is perfect." (Matthew 5:43-46,48)

Jesus' teaching on love for enemies means that his followers are to stay off the continuum of violence entirely.

Jesus' followers are never to engage in or support the violence of retaliation, retribution, and vengeance. Jesus teaches:
> "You have heard that it was said, 'An eye for an eye and a tooth for a tooth.' But I say to you, Do not resist an evildoer. But if anyone strikes you on the right cheek, turn the other also." (Matthew 5:38-39)

By building a movement based on love and nonviolence, Jesus is spreading a holistic alternative to Patriarchy—the "kingdom or commonwealth" of God on Earth. The movement is meant to undermine and replace patriarchal civilizations which are based on exploitation and so-called "justified violence."

> No violence is justified—not even in defense of Jesus. "Then they came and laid hands on Jesus and arrested him. Suddenly, one of those with Jesus put his hand on his sword, drew it, and struck the slave of the high priest, cutting off his ear. Then Jesus said to him, 'Put your sword back into its place; for all who take the sword will perish by the sword. Do you think that I cannot appeal to my Father [/ Mother], and [God] will at once send me more than twelve legions of angels?'" (Matthew 26:50b-53)

Jesus rejects being defended by violence. That would undermine his mission and strategy of love and nonviolence. So Jesus pays the price of his commitment to nonviolence and opposition to patriarchal leaders and rulers. Jesus is arrested, tortured, and crucified. But the agony of "Christ crucified" is followed by the resurrection—and the continuing call to follow Jesus on the path of love and nonviolence.

Patriarchal civilizations are bringing the world to ruin. They are based on lies, illusions, deceptions, and fraudulent world views. Patriarchal capitalism, in the fossil fuel era, has produced an enormous amount of wealth and material goods to provide for and satisfy affluent consumers. Patriarchal culture and society promotes and idolizes affluent lifestyles that have achieved the so-called "good life." But seeking and living the affluent good life is really living a lie. Patriarchal capitalism, with the support of police and military forces, has been maximizing the exploitation of natural resources. The mining of fossil fuels and precious metals has torn the Earth asunder, metaphorically raping the Earth, despoiling the environment, leaving a wake of pollution and degraded ecosystems, and propelling climate chaos. Propping up patriarchal civilization and patriarchal capitalism with "clean energy" is also a false path since it still upholds the lies of the affluent and materialistic good life. Patriarchal capitalism is at enmity with God and nature. Living the lie leads humanity further down the path of death and destruction.

It is Jesus' mission, along with his disciples, to not only overcome Patriarchy but to save the physical world including all of nature. Jesus said, "I came that they may have life and have it abundantly." (John 10:10) The life that Jesus offers reconnects people with God and Spirit, with the poor people of the Earth, and with nature. A result of this spiritual awakening and harmony is abundance. God's New Creation brings new life and abundance.

The disciple and apostle Paul writes about the ongoing travail of the natural world and the hope for a brighter future.

> "For the creation waits with eager longing for the revealing of the children of God…in hope that the creation itself will be set free from its bondage to decay and will obtain the freedom of the glory of the children of God. We know that the whole creation has been groaning in labor pains until now; and not only the creation, but we ourselves who have the first fruits of the Spirit, groan inwardly while we wait for adoption, the redemption of our bodies." (Romans 8:19-23)

The liberation and renewal of humanity is tied together with the liberation and renewal of the natural world with its many plants and species which are suffering under Patriarchy. All things are connected. And the only true hope for accomplishing this liberation and renewal is through Jesus and his discipleship/liberation movement.

Footnotes

1. Mark Berman, Lenny Bernstein, Dan Keating, Andrew Ba Tran, Artur Galocha, Washington Post, "The staggering scope of U.S. gun deaths," <u>Star Tribune</u>, July 10, 2022.
2. Julie Bosman, Kate Taylor, Tim Arango, NY Times, "Mass killers often bear hatred of women," <u>Star Tribune</u>, August 11, 2019.

3. Andres Resendez, <u>The Other Slavery: The Uncovered Story of Indian Enslavement in America</u>, Mariner Books, NY, 2016, pp. 3,5,6,270.
4. MN Historical Society, "American Indian Boarding Schools," <u>Duluth Reader</u>, March 22, 2018.
5. Peter Smith, AP, "U.S. churches confront traumatic legacy of Native schools," <u>Star Tribune</u>, July 23, 2021.
6. Brenda J. Child, <u>Native Universe: Voices of Indian America</u>, Gerald McMaster & Clifford E. Trafzer, editors, National Museum of the American Indian, Smithsonian Institution, National Geographic Society, Wash. D.C., 2004, p. 164.
7. Brenda J. Child, "To honor our native ancestors, get their history right," <u>Star Tribune</u>, July 30, 2021.
8. Jessica Washington, Fuller Project, "Legacy of fear lives on for Native families," <u>Star Tribune</u>, January 25, 2022.
9. Briana Bierschbach, "Tribes get new tool to battle sex crimes," <u>Star Tribune</u>, March 20, 2022.
10. Josh Boak, AP, "Biden marks Armenian genocide," <u>Star Tribune</u>, April 25, 2022.
11. John Rash, "World food supply may be the next casualty," <u>Star Tribune</u>, April 17, 2022.
12. Amnesty International, quoted in <u>SCARS ACROSS HUMANITY</u>, Elaine Storkey, p. 136.
13. Elaine Storkey, <u>SCARS ACROSS HUMANITY</u>, 2018, pp. 137-138.
14. Mary Daly, <u>Gyn / Ecology: The Metaethics of Radical Feminism</u>, Deacon Press, Boston, 1978, p. 361.
15. Rukmini Callimachi, NY Times, "Escaped ISIL captives reveal sex slavery system," <u>Star Tribune</u>, August 14, 2015.
16. Muneeza Naqvi, AP, "Perilous journey is their last hope," <u>Star Tribune</u>, September 6, 2017.
17. Kristen Gelineau, AP, "Rape used against Rohingya," <u>Star Tribune</u>, December 17, 2017.
18. Lara Jakes, NY Times, "Myanmar acts 'genocide'," <u>Star Tribune</u>, March 22, 2022.
19. Steve Andreasen, "Carnage in Ethiopia, too, merits world's attention," <u>Star Tribune</u>, April 13, 2022.
20. Cara Anna, AP, "Sexual violence shatters Tigray," <u>Star Tribune</u>, August 12, 2021.
21. Giulia Paravicini, Reuters, "Nearly half the people in Ethiopia's Tigray need food aid," <u>Duluth News Tribune</u>, August 20, 2022.
22. Sarah Kaplan, Washington Post, "A Call To Defuse 'Climate Time Bomb'," <u>Star Tribune</u>, March 21, 2023.

23. Kristine Phillips, Washington Post, "Scientists say Earth on path to a mass extinction," Star Tribune, July 23, 2017.
24. Jennifer Bjorhus, "Extinction threat 'quite alarming'," Star Tribune, July 19, 2022.
25. Jennifer Bjorhus, "Race Against Extinction," Star Tribune, September 4, 2022.
26. Corinne Purtill, LA Times, "How wildfires led to mass extinction eons ago," Star Tribune, August 7, 2022.
27. Seth Borenstein, AP, "We're all in big trouble," Star Tribune, September 26, 2019.
28. Sarah Kaplan, Washington Post, "The Amazon rain forest is losing its ability to bounce back," Star Tribune, March 9, 2022.
29. Henry Fountain, NY Times, "Despite pledges, forests keep falling," Star Tribune, May 1, 2022.
30. Erika Veidis, Jamie Hansen, Washington Post, "Schoolchildren connect plastics to health," Star Tribune, April 3, 2022.
31. Amanda Little, "A 'baby bust' may be welcome in a hot, hungry world," Star Tribune, May 12, 2021.
32. Sarah Kaplan, Washington Post, "A Call To Defuse 'Climate Time Bomb'," Star Tribune, March 21, 2023.
33. Mira Rojanasakul, Christopher Flavelle, Blacki Migliozzi, Eli Murray, NY Times, "Aquifers going dry next climate crisis," Star Tribune, August 30, 2023.
34. Somini Sengupta, NY Times, "Extreme heat could soon make some cities unlivable," Star Tribune, July 18, 2018.
35. Jamey Keaton and Seth Borenstein, AP, "Summer heat melts global records," Star Tribune, September 7, 2023.
36. Jeff Nesbit, This Is The Way The World Ends: How Droughts and Die-offs, Heat Waves and Hurricanes are Converging on America, Thomas Dunne Books, St. Martin's Press, New York, 2018, pp. 140,141,144,150,205,212,216,219.
37. Seth Borenstein, AP, "Sea Levels To Rise Sharply," Star Tribune, August 30, 2022.
38. Seth Borenstein, AP, "Historic ice collapse in Antarctica," Star Tribune, March 27, 2022.

Chapter 8

Patriarchy and Institutional Religion

The big-picture context for every problem, issue, or topic is a very broad understanding of Patriarchy. The basic premise of Patriarchy is male dominance and female subordination, resulting in hierarchy, inequality, oppression, and violence. Patriarchal societies standardize and institutionalize patriarchal hierarchies, oppression, and violence.

Patriarchal societies are accompanied with supporting patriarchal myths, philosophies, religions, traditions, and laws. These supporting patriarchal ideologies work to deeply indoctrinate people and deeply entrench human societies in Patriarchy. Patriarchy can be described as a "social totality," enveloping all people and institutions in a patriarchal milieu. All of this makes the overcoming of Patriarchy very difficult and points to the need for a human & divine Messiah to help humanity.

So, why are religions so popular throughout history? Human beings are naturally spiritual beings—with a deep inner connection to God—through the "spirit of life" within every living human being. "Wholesomeness" for human beings includes a close spiritual connection with God who is the source of life. Human beings have a natural longing and desire for knowing God and for spiritual enlightenment. Religions are an expression of this natural human longing for knowing God, knowing a supreme being, knowing "truth," knowing the "meaning of life," and knowing a permanent basis for moral and ethical laws. Religions, with their purported connection to God, are supposed to improve life, guide people towards a life of "fruitfulness" and bounty, explain and alleviate human suffering, bring personal empowerment, increase human cooperation, provide hope for salvation and immortality (life after death), and provide some hope for justice and liberation on Earth (a "new creation" or utopia). For many thousands of years human beings have sought to know God, to know if God is powerful, and, if so, to access or influence God's power. Numerous spiritualities and religions have arisen—but within the big-picture context of Patriarchy.

Patriarchy has ruled human civilizations for many thousands of years. Patriarchy "fragments the whole." Patriarchy works to separate humans from God, fragmenting the internal connection between body and spirit. Patriarchy misdirects and exploits the natural human longing for physical and spiritual wholeness. Patriarchal fragmentation occurs through: people's internal suppression of natural spiritual longings, substitution of addictions for real relationship with God, striving for more materialistic goods and wealth, various forms of oppression & violence & trauma, and, very commonly, misguided patriarchal religions.

Patriarchal male leaders, in particular, have taken advantage of people's natural spiritual longings. Many patriarchal male leaders have realized the value of various patriarchal religions in controlling and ruling people and providing powerful ideologies for guiding different gender roles and class roles. (Fragment, divide, and conquer.) For a long time, various patriarchal religions have led people astray by promoting allegiance and obedience to patriarchal leaders, rituals, symbols, and institutions. Throughout human history humans have invented thousands of gods and goddesses, developed many patriarchal religions, devised innumerable rituals and ceremonies, and created a class of patriarchal religious intermediaries who purportedly specialize in connecting "ordinary" humans with the gods and goddesses they promote. The main beneficiary has been the patriarchal ruling class.

Patriarchal religions deceive people and lead people to believe in many things that are not true. People can have very deeply held internal beliefs that are not true. Individuals can collude in patriarchal religions through self-deception and large numbers of people can experience mass delusion—all the while fervently believing that their deeply-internalized beliefs are true. Thousands of false gods and goddesses would attest to this (if they could).

Patriarchal religions represent a very powerful influence over society and help to establish deep-rooted oppression of girls and women. Patriarchal religions can tie "God" (or gods and goddesses) to a so-called "natural order" which supports male dominance and female subordination. This so-called "natural order," since it is supposedly instituted by God, makes the prevailing patriarchal order seem unchangeable and permanent. The resulting oppression and abuses of females, in particular, can go on for millennia.

Over time, major religions can become "institutionalized." "Institutionalized religion" is a religion with designated religious buildings, a clerical class (with positions and/or titles for religious leaders), and usually a legitimizing relationship with the state or with local and national political leaders. Since Patriarchy rules human civilizations, all institutional religions are patriarchal. The patriarchal clerical-religious class exercises elite control over religious services and rituals, theology (sermons, God-language, creeds, dogma, and interpretation of scripture), and symbolic "access to God" (via the above controls and a fixed religious location). Institutional religions may have an all-male clerical-religious class—or they may integrate women into leadership positions—without losing their essential patriarchal character. Institutional religions maintain religious hierarchies and patriarchal theology, often receive benefits and privileges from the state, and, in general, legitimize various social hierarchies.

Institutional patriarchal religions can be found all over the world. Patriarchy is so dominant that it could be described: "Patriarchy is itself the prevailing religion of the entire planet....All of the so-called religions legitimating patriarchy are mere sects subsumed under its vast umbrella/canopy. They are essentially similar despite the variations. All—from buddhism and hinduism to islam, judaism, christianity, to secular derivatives such as freudianism, jungianism, marxism, and maoism—are infrastructures of the edifice of patriarchy." *1 Mary Daly

Can the "true God" be found within the "husk" of patriarchal institutional religions? We might consider, in the context of the patriarchal history of religions and civilizations, how the true, living God is going to work to overcome Patriarchy and bring salvation, justice, and liberation to the whole world. How is God going to do it? What is God's strategy?

<u>God/Jesus Against Patriarchy</u>

The key assumption and starting point, from my faith perspective, is that Jesus is the unique Messiah (leader of God's liberation movement) and the unique Son of God (both human and divine). Then some evidence can be considered: the Hebrew-Judaic-Christian history of God's struggle against the power of Patriarchy. Since the history and the evidence are so immense only a little will be presented here. Also, it is important to realize that God is working under some self-imposed restraints. These restraints restrict God's use of God's infinite Spirit-power. What are some of these restraints?

God has made a very deep commitment to human freedom. God has granted "free will" to humans, giving humans freedom to make choices and decisions without any divine interference. Humans have free will to make decisions, to reflect on those decisions, and to live with the consequences of those decisions. Humans have the freedom of faith, of freely choosing what they will believe in, without any coercion or imposition from God. Humans have the freedom to discern (and to do or not do) God's will based upon whatever faith and beliefs they have chosen. In a similar vein, humans have the freedom to make and pursue their own goals without any overbearing sense of God's judgment. And humans have the freedom to use their incredible brains and consciousness in a stagnating or expanding way to develop their beings and characters according to their faith and lifestyles. Humans have the freedom to follow Jesus and "enter into God's kingdom or commonwealth on Earth." No person can "enter" through coercion or force—only through free will, free choice. Human partnership with God must be freely chosen.

Under these self-imposed restraints, God's handiwork is usually hidden and God's Spirit is unseen. The immanence and presence of God is everywhere—but it is not yet obvious or scientifically provable. God is always involved in creation and the ongoing evolutionary process of the whole universe—but humans must seek to develop their own faith and to know God. However, God's invisibility to humans changed dramatically, at least for some people of faith, with God's sending of Jesus to live among humanity. Through Jesus, God revealed a path for humans to know God deeply, to clearly understand God's will, and to influence and access God's Spirit-power. Since the time of Jesus the visibility and understanding of the true God should have grown rapidly...except for the countervailing power of Patriarchy.

Long before God sent Jesus, God was working to call people out of Patriarchy and to form an alternative. This history is partially recorded in the Bible in the Old Testament (OT).

However, the Bible was composed within patriarchal history by many different authors and contains different and competing theologies of God. Much of the Bible was inspired by God and has a bent towards justice and liberation. And much of the Bible was written to support Patriarchy and contains great distortions of God and historical lies. History is usually written to support the ruling class—by the pens of those who serve their patriarchal rulers. The great OT prophet Jeremiah regularly lambasted Israel's male political and religious leaders:

> "How can you say, 'We are wise, and the law of the LORD [Yahweh] is with us,' when, in fact, the false pen of the scribes has made it into a lie? The wise shall be put to shame…since they have rejected the word of the LORD, what wisdom is in that?....from the least to the greatest everyone is greedy for unjust gain; from prophet to priest everyone deals falsely." (Jeremiah 8:8-10)

"The false pen of the scribes" distorted religious texts and provided patriarchal "wisdom" which was absolutely not the wisdom of God. In this context of patriarchal distortions of scripture, reading the Bible requires much discernment.

In the OT God began "small" in the historical battle to overcome Patriarchy. Patriarchal civilizations filled the Earth with patriarchal hierarchies, inequalities, exploitation, oppression, and violence. But God called Abraham and Sarah to obey God's voice and to "come out" of Patriarchy by leaving their homeland and their family ties in order to become sojourners. This very small beginning came with a big promise. Abraham and Sarah were promised innumerable descendants, foretelling the rise of people of faith in God who hear and obey God's voice. Of course, Abraham and Sarah continued to be immersed in patriarchal lands and cultures—and they themselves were very patriarchal. Nevertheless, it was a small start.

Perhaps the greatest event in the OT, and the most formative event for establishing the tribal commonwealth of Israel, was God's leadership after Abraham's and Sarah's descendants fell into slavery in Egypt. Abraham's and Sarah's descendants multiplied in Egypt, leading Pharaoh to order the Hebrew midwives Shiprah and Puah to kill Hebrew baby boys. It was sort of a strong-armed patriarchal "solution" to the threat of too many Hebrews—just kill the baby boys.

> "But the midwives feared God; they did not do as the king of Egypt commanded them, but they let the boys live." (Exodus 1:17)

The midwives preferred God's leadership and defied Pharaoh's order. One male baby who survived, Moses, obeyed God's voice and followed God's guidance. Moses asked for the name of God and God answered, "I am who I am" (or "I am who I will be"). From this answer YHWH, or Yahweh, is derived. Unlike other gods and goddesses this God that Moses identified as "I am/Yahweh" does not favor the rich and powerful, but instead cares about the Hebrew slaves.

> "Then the LORD [Yahweh] said, 'I have observed the misery of my people who are in Egypt; I have heard their cry on account of their taskmasters. Indeed, I know their sufferings, and I have come down to deliver them from the Egyptians.'" (Exodus 3:7-8a)

So this unseen God, through Moses' nonviolent and courageous leadership, and with "signs and wonders," liberated the Hebrew slaves from Egypt.

Freeing the Hebrew slaves from Egypt becomes a distinguishing feature of "I am/Yahweh"—the God of liberation. Yet the freed Hebrew slaves found themselves in the wilderness, without a homeland, and with very little understanding of who God is. Patriarchy still prevailed and no strong alternative to it was known. In the wilderness there were opportunities for the Hebrews to learn dependence and reliance upon God and to learn God's will for equality and justice. But it didn't all go down well. Nevertheless, Moses led the people into a covenant relationship with "I am/Yahweh" and God's ten commandments. The first commandment reads:

> "I am the LORD [Yahweh] your God, who brought you out of the land of Egypt, out of the house of slavery; you shall have no other gods before me." (Exodus 20:2)

The Hebrews are called to follow "I am/Yahweh" only—for "I am/Yahweh" is the only God who enters into patriarchal history on the side of the slaves and works for liberation of the oppressed.

God began small with the call of Abraham and Sarah. God's call expanded to the freed Hebrew slaves after their mass exodus from Egypt:

> "If you obey my voice and keep my covenant, you shall be my treasured possession out of all the peoples. Indeed,

the whole earth is mine, but you shall be for me a priestly kingdom and a holy nation." (Exodus 19:5-6)

The liberated Hebrew slaves were called to a path of obedience to "I am/Yahweh" and, collectively, to be a nation of justice and righteousness—different from all other oppressive patriarchal kingdoms and nations. Collectively they were called to be a "holy nation"—without patriarchal hierarchies and inequalities. So, while the above quote uses some patriarchal language—"priestly" and "kingdom," both of which represent patriarchal male-dominated hierarchies—the Hebrew people were meant to have neither. They were to remember their former status as foreigners and slaves. They were meant to rise higher and, collectively, to be a whole people/nation of justice for all.

Patriarchy, however, was still pervasive and the turning of the Hebrews to follow "I am/Yahweh" was still shallow. The Hebrews established an all-male religious priestly class and then a male-dominated kingly monarchy. These were major steps of moving away from God's leadership and toward reintegration into Patriarchy.

This establishment of an all-male religious priestly class enshrined discrimination against females, contributing to systemic oppression. The all-male priestly class propagated laws and statutes fraudulently in the names of Moses and God, which "locked-in" patriarchal biases and unjust codes. The patriarchal priestly class "fragmented the people," created divisions among the people, and acted as intermediaries between God and everyone else. They supported a false, hierarchical "natural order" and adhered to a self-serving "purity and pollution" system. Part of the "purity codes" required people to regularly bring grains, birds, and animals to the priests to be "sacrificed" and, oftentimes, consumed by the priests. Well did the great OT prophet Jeremiah rail against the Hebrews moving away from God.

"Thus says the LORD [Yahweh] of hosts, the God of Israel: Add your burnt offerings to your sacrifices, and eat the flesh. For in the day that I brought your ancestors out of the land of Egypt, I did not speak to them or command them concerning burnt offerings and sacrifices. But this command I gave them, 'Obey my voice, and I will be your God, and you shall be my people; and walk only in the way that I command you, so that it may be well with you.' Yet they did not obey or incline their ear, but in the stubbornness of their evil will they walked in their own counsels, and looked backward rather than forward....They did worse than their ancestors did." (Jeremiah 7:21-24,26)

In the above passage Jeremiah rebuked the male Hebrew leaders. Instead of obeying the voice of God they prioritized "burnt offerings and sacrifices" and improvised their own counsels and courses of action.

Expiation and Atonement

Burnt offerings and sacrifices stem from the purity and pollution system and from patriarchal theologies of "expiation and atonement." The patriarchal theologies of expiation and atonement have had long-lasting detrimental consequences. These theologies are a centerpiece of both the Jewish and Christian religions. These patriarchal theologies have greatly distorted the image of God and knowledge of the true God. These theologies promote the belief that a penalty must be paid to atone for both the individual and collective "sins and/or uncleanness" of the people. These patriarchal theologies teach that expiation via the "shedding of blood" through bird and animal sacrifices in the OT and through Jesus' execution on the cross in the New Testament were necessary to appease and satisfy a strict, judgmental, and demanding holy God in heaven by "covering over the sins of the people with holy blood." (Leviticus 17:10-12) But these theologies from the minds of men are patriarchal projections which fashion an authoritarian and unmerciful god of their own making. The OT prophet Hosea prophesied: "For I desire steadfast love and not sacrifice, the knowledge of God rather than burnt offerings." (Hosea 6:6) And Jesus rebuked some self-righteous male leaders of his time: "Go and learn what this means, 'I desire mercy, not sacrifice.'" (Matthew 9:13)

The patriarchal theologies of expiation and atonement justify and support killing and the "shedding of blood" which is the basis for patriarchal governance and military forces. They turn Jesus' execution at the hands of patriarchal leaders into a theologically-justified bloody "sacrifice" required by God to atone for people's sins. They subordinate social justice and liberation to the cultist legal requirement of a purity and pollution system under the supervision of a clerical class. They serve to pacify the people and uphold a patriarchal, hierarchal social order.

The patriarchal theologies of expiation and atonement can mislead believers about God's will for their life-paths.

> "The myth of expiation strives to give meaning to suffering by postulating that all guilt deserves a proportionate punishment....the expiatory vision of redemption....sanctions a religious culture of shame. The compulsive need to punish others and/or ourselves gains legitimacy from the motif of expiation....Instead of crushing the life out of sinners by demanding expiation, divine love as revealed in Jesus opens up the possibility of new life unceasingly. This is what Christianity means, at the very least by its belief in 'the forgiveness of sins.'" *2
> John F. Haught

Theologies of expiation and atonement can lead to: seeking retribution against others, seeking reparations from others, lingering guilt and regrets, shame, passivity, and little or no changes in one's life-path. However, Jesus' forgiveness of sins is is qualitatively different in its response to sinfulness. Jesus' forgiveness of sins is simple and direct and contrasts significantly from calls for penalties, penance, and submission to patriarchal religious and legal systems. While Jesus offers love and forgiveness to all, most people are not ready for it.*3 For repentant people who recognize their sinfulness and desire healing for themselves and for others, Jesus' forgiveness involves wiping the slate clean, getting a new start, and changing the direction of one's life-path. It involves looking forward and not backward—and not getting stuck in the muck of past sinfulness. Jesus is always calling people to move forward and to realign themselves with God's will/path by seeking first "God's kingdom or commonwealth on Earth." Jesus' call is to get moving forward on the life-path of liberation and overcoming Patriarchy.

Return to OT History

Another major step away from God's leadership occurred when all the male elders of Israel came to the prophet and judge Samuel

> "and said to him, 'You are old and your sons do not follow in your ways; appoint for us, then, a king to govern us, like other nations.'" (1 Samuel 8:5)

Instead of breaking away from Patriarchy and becoming an alternative to it under "I am/Yahweh's" leadership, Israel kept conforming more and more to the ways of Patriarchy. By choosing to become a monarchy under a male king like all the nations, Israel essentially rejected God's leadership in favor of a more standard patriarchal rulership. Of course Israel was already deeply patriarchal and this step just further integrated it into Patriarchy.

Israel's time of monarchy and division into two kingdoms was a drawn-out exercise in the futility of trying to maintain the facade of loyalty and obedience to "I am/Yahweh" while in practice conforming to the oppressive, violent, and idolatrous ways of Patriarchy. Centralized power under a king resulted in greater oppression, economic inequalities, and class divisions. King Solomon built his royal palace and the temple adjacent to it with slave labor. (1 Kings 9:15) While it is not stated explicitly how active King Solomon's "dick" was, he supported the sexual exploitation of females for "among his wives were seven hundred princesses and three hundred concubines [female sex slaves]." (1 Kings 11:3) The temple in Jerusalem functioned to centralize religious worship under an all-male priestly class which, in turn, was loyal to a patriarchal ruling class. The divided kingdoms of Israel and Judah were no longer under God's leadership and protection but, like other small nations, were subject to the rise and fall of neighboring empires. The OT prophet Hosea prophesied about their plight:

> "Where now is your king, that he may save you? Where in all your cities are your rulers, of whom you said, 'Give me a king and rulers'? I gave you a king in my anger, and I took him away in my wrath." (Hosea 13:10-11)

For the divided kingdoms of Israel and Judah there was no escape from being conquered by the empires of Assyria or Babylonia.

So, Patriarchy prevails. What is "I am/Yahweh's" next move in the struggle to overcome Patriarchy and bring justice and liberation to the whole world? So far, in the OT, God has developed some history of liberation, knowledge of God, a permanent moral law (the ten commandments), and prophetic messages for the joining of faith with justice that provide much context for God's biggest move ever—the sending of a Messiah. But it doesn't happen right away.

The northern kingdom of Israel was conquered by Assyria around 722 B.C.E. The southern kingdom of Judah was decisively conquered by Babylonia around 587 B.C.E. Later on

Israel reconstituted itself as a patriarchal nation and as a religious people with a second temple. But it was dominated by foreign powers. Then a violent revolution under the leadership of Judas "Maccabeus" against the Seleucids/Syrians was successful and around 164 B.C.E. the temple was "cleansed" and dedicated. (And thus Jews every year remember this successful violent revolution and celebrate the eight-day Feast of Hanukkah (Dedication) or Festival of Lights). A modicum of independence was achieved. The patriarchal Hasmonean rulership commenced.

Around 63 B.C.E. General Pompey conquered and annexed Judea and made it a Roman province. The power of the Roman Empire extended over all of Israel. It was under the domination of the Roman Empire when the greatest intervention of God occurred—the sending of the Messiah. It began small and was well-disguised. It began with the pregnancy of a young betrothed woman, Mary, without the involvement of any man or "male seed." In their patriarchal society it was scandalous for a woman to get pregnant except by her husband. So Mary, and her first-born son Jesus, had to bear the scorn of a patriarchal society (and without longstanding support from Mary's husband Joseph who disappears from biblical texts).

The birth of Jesus has humble origins—in an animal stable in Bethlehem—as Mary and Joseph were traveling to be registered in their home region according to a decree by Roman Emperor Augustus. Around 5 B.C.E., while King Herod was still the Roman-appointed ruler of Palestine, Jesus was born. The birth of Jesus to a poor couple was seemingly insignificant. Yet King Herod became alarmed when magi traveling from the East reported to him that they were traveling to worship the newborn king of the Jews. Consequently, King Herod ordered that all male children up to 2 years old in Bethlehem and the surrounding vicinity be slain. But Mary and Joseph and Jesus had already left the area. King Herod's response provided a clear view to the strong-armed and often brutal realities of Patriarchy.

After King Herod died in 4 B.C.E. some of the Jewish people violently revolted against Roman rule. Roman legions came and crushed the rebellion. They burned down the prominent city of Sepphoris in Galilee, located just a few miles from the small town of Nazareth where Jesus grew up. It was another reminder of the strong-armed methods of patriarchal rulership.

At about the age of 30 Jesus began his active full-time ministry. Jesus' ministry was an offshoot of John the Baptist's movement which heightened Jewish expectations for an imminent Messiah. Jesus' ministry began small, with just a few disciples and with a local focus on the people of Israel. Jesus called men and women to leave behind their patriarchal families and to form a new inclusive and egalitarian family centered around Jesus.

> "Then his mother and his brothers came; and standing outside, they sent to him and called him. A crowd was sitting around him; and they said to him, 'Your mother and your brothers and sisters are outside, asking for you.' And he replied, 'Who are my mother and my brothers?' And looking at those who sat around him, he said, 'Here are my mother and my brothers! Whoever does the will of God is my brother and sister and mother.'" (Mark 3:31-35)

Tellingly, Jesus' new family leaves out the patriarchal position of "father."

Jesus called women to a higher consciousness—and to respond to a higher calling.

> "...a woman in the crowd raised her voice and said to him, 'Blessed is the womb that bore you and the breasts that nursed you!' But he said, 'Blessed rather are those who hear the word of God and obey it!'" (Luke 11:27-28)

Jesus lifts up for women the higher priority of hearing the word of God and doing God's will.

> "Now as they went on their way, he entered a certain village, where a woman named Martha welcomed him into her home. She had a sister named Mary, who sat at the Lord's feet and listened to what he was saying. But Martha was distracted by her many tasks; so she came to him and asked, 'Lord, do you not care that my sister has left me to do all the work by myself? Tell her then to help me.' But the Lord answered her, 'Martha, Martha, you are worried and distracted by many things; there is need of only one thing. Mary has chosen the better part, which will not be taken away from her.'" (Luke 10:38-42)

Women are called to be followers and disciples of Jesus—for surely Patriarchy will not be overcome by men alone as centuries of evidence attest.

In Jesus' discipleship/liberation movement women could become teachers, prophets, and evangelistic messengers, i.e., apostles. Women were the first witnesses of Jesus' resurrection and thereby the first disciples/apostles sent by Jesus to spread the good news. In all the gospel accounts Jesus' highest praise was given to a woman.

> "While he was at Bethany in the house of Simon the leper, as he sat at the table, a woman came with an alabaster jar of very costly ointment of nard, and she broke open the jar and poured the ointment on his head. But some were there who said to one another in anger, 'Why was the ointment wasted in this way? For this ointment could have been sold for more than three hundred denarii, and the money given to the poor.' And they scolded her. But Jesus said, 'Let her alone; why do you trouble her? She has performed a good service for me. For you always have the poor with you, and you can show kindness to them whenever you wish; but you will not always have me. She has done what she could; she has anointed my body beforehand for its burial. Truly I tell you, wherever the good news is proclaimed in the whole world, what she has done will be told in remembrance of her.'" (Mark 14:3-9)

Jesus' affirmation and praise of this unnamed (in the Gospel of Mark) female disciple runs counter to the scolding she received. The woman boldly takes the initiative and anoints Jesus. She is criticized and rebuked, probably by male disciples of Jesus, because they see a higher priority of selling the expensive ointment and giving the money to poor people. But Jesus intervenes and corrects the male disciples misreading of this act of faith. The woman made a timely gift of faith and love to Jesus. Jesus is always to be at the center of discipleship—but his physical body would not remain present much longer. Jesus affirms giving to poor people—but the higher priority is keeping his body or spiritual being at the center of discipleship. The woman anointed Jesus thus affirming in faith that Jesus is the Messiah, i.e., the "anointed one." The ointment prepared Jesus for his impending crucifixion, death, and burial. Thus the woman affirmed Jesus and the confounding message of "Christ crucified" —a message Jesus repeatedly taught his male disciples and which they failed to understand. (Mark 8:31,9:31-32) Jesus foresees that his still small liberation movement will greatly expand—to the whole world—and that female discipleship, like the example of this woman, must be proclaimed and supported.

Of course, Jesus called men to become his followers and disciples. Men have tremendous responsibility for upholding Patriarchy—and must play a key role in working to overcome it. To "restore the whole" both men and women must join together in following Jesus. But men's new role may not come easily to them. Despite Jesus' teachings, the male disciples were not ready for Jesus' execution and departure. They did not listen and understand as well as the above unnamed female disciple.

In Jesus' day Jewish men had expectations for the coming of a "warrior messiah" who would lead a violent revolution to overthrow their Roman oppressors and establish an independent Israel after the model of King David's powerful patriarchal kingdom. But Jesus taught against this.

"And he began to teach them that the [Human One] must suffer many things, and be rejected by the elders and the chief priests and the scribes, and be killed, and after three days rise again. And he said this plainly. And Peter took him, and began to rebuke him. But turning and seeing his disciples, he rebuked Peter, and said, 'Get behind me, Satan! For you are not on the side of God, but of men.' And he called to him the multitude with his disciples, and said to them, 'If any man would come after me, let him deny himself and take up his cross and follow me. For whoever would save his life will lose it; and whoever loses his life for my sake and the gospel's will save it. For what does it profit a man, to gain the whole world and forfeit his life? For what can a man give in return for his life? For whoever is ashamed of me and of my words in this adulterous and sinful generation, of him will the [Human One] also be ashamed.'" (Mark 8:31-38) Revised Standard Version

Violent revolution, historically led and fought by men, is a violent patriarchal method of seeking to gain greater dominative power. Even if the revolution is successful, and even if the male fighters "gain the whole world," the fighters "forfeit their life" by killing others (under God's judgment) and there is nothing they can give in return for their life. The way of Patriarchy is a dead end. The way of Jesus is the way of love and nonviolence. It involves carrying "the cross"—and not weapons for warfare. The cross represented the brutal Roman method of crucifixion and execution and was used to put down any type of rebellion against their rule. This was a difficult teaching for Jesus' first male disciples. They were filled with expectations for a "warrior messiah" and, like Peter (John 18:10), more than willing to take part in male "warrior heroism." This lesson of Jesus continues to be particularly difficult for male Christians, many of whom proudly join the armed forces and carry deadly weapons.

Another difficult lesson for male disciples was Jesus' teaching and example of "servant leadership," which runs contrary to patriarchal society. (Mark 10:42-45) For male disciples of Jesus this means overcoming male dominance, male privilege, male competition and ambitions for positions and titles, and the selfish pride and ego that lingers on.

Jesus' movement began small but he quickly drew large crowds. Within Israel, Jesus faced very strong opposition from the all-male religious leaders. They viewed Jesus as a dire threat.
"The chief priests and the Pharisees called a meeting of the council, and said, 'What are we to do? This man is performing many signs. If we let him go on like this, everyone will believe in him, and the Romans will come and destroy both our holy place and our nation.'...So from that day on they planned to put him to death." (John 11:47-48,53)
The patriarchal Jewish religious leaders conspired with the Roman authorities to arrest, torture, and execute Jesus.

The brutal violence and power of Patriarchy, in the guise of the Roman Empire, brought an end to Jesus' ministry and life in Israel. This would have been the end of the story, with Patriarchy prevailing, if it wasn't for Jesus' resurrection. But Jesus' resurrection means that the gospel, the good news of Jesus the Messiah, continues—and the movement's field of operation has grown much larger. Henceforth, God's efforts to overcome Patriarchy are not narrowly focused on Israel but now include the whole world. Jesus' life, ministry, crucifixion, and resurrection provide confirmation that God is "all-in" in the historical struggle to overcome Patriarchy. But with Jesus' physical and visible body no longer present more responsibility falls on followers and disciples of Jesus to carry forward the participatory, Spirit-empowering, and liberating movement.

How will Jesus' movement fare? The patriarchal, polytheistic, slave-based, and militaristic Roman Empire put Jesus' movement to the test. For a period of time in the beginning the movement fared quite well, growing and spreading profusely within the Roman Empire. Despite times of persecution and some mass killings the movement remained largely nonviolent and pacifist, remaining steadfast to Jesus' way of love and nonviolence. The movement attracted many poor and oppressed people—and even some people from the privileged classes. A text in Paul's letter to the Galatians may reflect a part of early Christian baptismal liturgies which emphasized social equality and justice.

> "As many of you as were baptized into Christ have clothed yourselves with Christ. There is no longer Jew or Greek, there is no longer slave or free, there is no longer male and female; for all of you are one in Christ Jesus." (Galatians 3:27-28)

Adult baptism brought the oppressed and the formerly privileged into a liberation movement characterized by social equality and the absence of social hierarchies. However, not all was going well.

The patriarchal Roman Empire could not stamp out Jesus' movement simply through persecution and violent state repression. Eventually, however, Patriarchy was able to reassert itself over the movement due to a combination of *internal corruption* of the movement and then, in the 4th century, *external co-optation* of the movement by Roman Emperor Constantine.

The *internal corruption* of the movement by patriarchal impulses occurred as Jesus was not physically present to correct wayward male disciples, in particular. Jesus' physical departure opened the door for others to assert their leadership and authority. Consequently, the discipleship movement had many internal struggles over leadership and authority—with male leadership eventually prevailing decisively.

One pathway to affirming patriarchal male leadership was through recognizing the leadership position and authority of so-called "apostles." This was accompanied with affirming certain males as "apostles" and "silencing or erasing" females as apostles.

Another pathway for affirming patriarchal male leadership was by establishing recognized positions or "offices" within Christian communities. Positions were established primarily for male leaders: bishop/overseer, elder/presbyter/priest, and deacon.

> "The shift which took place in the second century was not a shift from charismatic leadership to institutional consolidation, but from charismatic and communal authority to an authority vested in local officers, who—in time—absorb not only the teaching authority of the prophet and apostle but also the decision-making power of the community. This shift is, at the same time, a shift from alternating leadership accessible to all the baptized to patriarchal leadership restricted to male heads of households." *4 Elisabeth Schussler Fiorenza

Jesus' movement became less egalitarian and more patriarchal and hierarchical.

Another pathway to affirming patriarchal male leadership was through controlling important Christian texts (or "scriptures") and editorially altering some texts. Some of Paul's writings were "doctored" or changed by later editors who added "interpolations" such as 1 Corinthians 14:34-35, which supported male dominance and female subordination. Some texts allegedly written by Paul are actually pseudepigrapha—texts fraudulently attributed to Paul and written by unknown writers—such as Colossians, Ephesians, 1 & 2 Timothy, and Titus.

Several texts, whose authorship is unknown, contain what are called "household codes"—and can be found in Ephesians, Colossians, 1 Timothy, 1 Peter, and Titus.

> "The basic form of this code consists of three pairs of reciprocal exhortations addressing the relationship between wife and husband, children and father, and slaves and masters. In each case, the socially subordinate first member of the pair is exhorted to obedience to the superordinate second." *5 Elisabeth Schussler Fiorenza

The writers/editors of the household codes sought to promote patriarchal relationships among Christians. By increasing conformity of the Christian movement to the dominant Greco-Roman society, the household codes functioned to reduce friction and conflict with the patriarchal society. The Christian movement was moving towards increasing re-integration with Patriarchy.

Internal corruption of Jesus' movement set it up for *external co-optation* by the ruling powers. Early in the 4th century, Roman Emperor Constantine legalized and promoted Christianity. Roman power promoted the patriarchal Christian church establishment and Christian doctrinal orthodoxy. Patriarchal Christianity eventually became the official religion of the Roman Empire.

> "After the toleration and legitimization of the Roman church between 313 and 330 AD, the emperor Theodosius, in 382 AD, declared it the only religion of Rome....
> The religious temptation finally triumphed in 382 AD, when Pope Damasus added the word "Roman' to the word 'Catholic' and then assumed the Roman title *Pontifex Maximus*." *6 William Durland

The partnership of church and state, of patriarchal Christianity with Roman power, was a major setback for Jesus' movement. With the protection and backing of state power the Roman Catholic Church began accumulating buildings, land, and wealth. The Church became an imperialistic religion which greatly extended its territorial dominion.

In Carthage, around 397, the official canon of written texts that formed the Christian New Testament were selected. These texts included the ones mentioned above that were tampered with to promote male dominance and female subordination. Also included were the four gospel texts of Matthew, Mark, Luke, and John, allegedly written by male apostles, which became the best enduring historical memories of Jesus' life, ministry, teachings, and practices. *7

Patriarchal, institutional Christianity took firm control over all the New Testament texts and their interpretations. An all-male clerical, priestly class presided and acted as intermediaries between the "laity" or "common Christians" and God. Adherence to patriarchal church doctrines and creeds became more important than believers' personal relationships with Jesus and direct personal empowerment through Jesus-Spirit-God. Patriarchal institutional churches emphasized church membership and attendance over real discipleship to Jesus. Patriarchal institutional churches became a substitute for more egalitarian grassroots communities.

The *internal corruption* of Jesus' movement primarily by ambitious patriarchal men and the *external co-optation* by patriarchal Roman rulers dealt major blows to Jesus' movement.

The dissipation of Jesus' movement shows some of the power and resiliency of Patriarchy.

In general, any religion that supports social hierarchies and so-called "justified violence" is dangerous and deadly. "Power corrupts and absolute power corrupts absolutely." The mix of patriarchal institutional religion with coercive and violent state power is toxic, particularly for females and minorities. Particularly bad is when a state becomes a theocracy— supposedly operating under a "god" while being ruled by a patriarchal clerical class or by other religious zealots. A theocracy will intensify state oppression and repression. It will intensify patriarchal ruling-class self-righteousness, authoritarianism, condescending paternalism and intolerance, while seeking to impose various religious views or moral codes on everyone, including rigid gender roles.

While a theocracy is certainly horrible, an alliance between "church and state" can also result in great levels of violence and evil. Patriarchal institutional Christianity, in alliance with the state, has been responsible for torrents of persecution, pogroms, inquisitions, witch hunts, widespread sexual abuses, crusades, wars, white settler colonialism, and genocide. Patriarchal institutional Christianity has revealed itself tens of millions of times to be more of an enemy of Jesus than a true representative of Jesus.

So, how does "I am/Yahweh," the God of liberation, deal with yet another setback? What is God's plan for moving forward now? The solution for overcoming Patriarchy remains the same. It does not change. The solution is through following Jesus and building and spreading Jesus' discipleship/liberation movement. This remains the solution for however long it takes. And it could take a long time because of the growth and dominance of patriarchal institutional Christianity. Institutional religion presents major obstacles and problems for moving forward. The re-forming and revival of Jesus' discipleship/liberation movement in a holistic form will take considerable time. In the meantime small new formations have occurred in new religious orders and in some monasteries and convents. God's Spirit is always working in individuals, small groups, households, small communities, and in anyone who, in some ways, is doing God's will. But "fragmented" efforts are less fruitful than "holistic" communal efforts.

So, moving forward, it would take many centuries before the Bible could be sufficiently printed so that it could get into the hands of more of the "laity." "Freeing up" the four New Testament gospels of "Matthew, Mark, Luke, and John" from clerical control was very important for refreshing people's memory and faith in Jesus. When the Christian Reformation began in the 16th century in Europe, many Christians broke away from the patriarchal Roman Catholic Church. But most of the leaders of the new Christian groups were men. Most Protestant (highlighting the word *protest*) groups, while breaking from the Roman Catholic Church, continued to support an alliance between church and state. Prominent Protestant leaders like Martin Luther, Ulrich Zwingli, and John Calvin

"completely rejected the notion of religious liberty. Catholics and Protestants alike agreed that dissenters had to be dealt with by force if they did not yield to persuasion." *8 Walter Klassen

The Anabaptists represented the radical part of the Reformation, breaking away from institutional Christianity and the state, and emphasizing a deep commitment to follow Jesus. The anabaptist practice of adult (re)baptism brought about a fierce backlash from church and state. Rulers, Catholics, and even Protestant reformers sought to capture and kill anabaptists. Thousands of anabaptists were imprisoned, tortured, drowned, burned at the stake, or beheaded. The fury of the backlash against the nonviolent anabaptists revealed, once again, how far patriarchal institutional Christianity had moved away from Jesus and his mission of universal liberation and the overcoming of Patriarchy.

Anabaptist groups and their descendants have included Hutterites, Mennonites, Amish, Brethren in Christ, and Bruderhof. They represented deep and strong commitments to Jesus. Yet, they were deeply steeped in Patriarchy and some were isolationist. While in some ways their witness was quite powerful, in other ways they revealed how hard it was to restart a holistic discipleship/liberation movement. Even more transformation was needed.

Because patriarchal institutional Christianity overlaid all things "Christian" with a patriarchal canopy, there was a great need for feminist movements. Feminist movements brought to light various forms of oppression of women and girls. Some feminists began to name patriarchy and expose and denounce some of its foundations and misogynistic practices. A feminist hermeneutic was essential for re-reading and reinterpreting both the Old and New Testaments. Only with feminist insights does it become clear that Jesus' mission was and is a mission to liberate both women and men from Patriarchy.

One could surmise that God's Spirit was working, in hidden ways, in various 20th century movements in America. The Catholic Worker movement emphasized small community formation, "gospel practices/works of mercy," hospitality, and nonviolent protests. Liberation theology emphasized God's "preferential option for the poor" and the formation of grassroots Christian base communities. The anti-Vietnam war and anti-nukes movements and Plowshares nuclear disarmament actions protested racist wars of aggression and genocidal threats. The civil rights movement exposed systemic racism and entrenched layers of segregation and discrimination. The American Indian Movement and other Native American protests exposed never-ending white settler colonialism and exploitation of Native peoples and lands. The gay liberation movement exposed heterosexism, homophobia, and society-wide discrimination against gays and lesbians. Environmental movements raised the alarms concerning air and land and water pollution and the harms being done to ecosystems and various species. The women's movement plus all these other movements provided educational and lifestyle-altering opportunities. They helped to raise people's consciousness and increase people's understanding of social justice and liberation.

Patriarchal Institutional Religious Abuses

Patriarchal institutional religions that prescribe male dominance and female subordination establish a powerful ideological foundation for patriarchal hierarchies, oppression, and violence against women and children. The abuses have been going on for millennia.

Clergy sexual abuses in the Roman Catholic Church in the U.S. and elsewhere have been an ongoing scandal for decades.
"French clergy sexually abused more than 200,000 children over the past 70 years, a major investigation released on [10-5-2021] found, and its authors said the

Catholic Church had turned a blind eye to the 'scourge' for too long. The church had shown 'deep, total and even cruel indifference for years,' protecting itself rather than victims of what was systemic abuse, said Jean-Marc Sauve, head of the commission that compiled the report. Most of the victims were boys, he said, many of them aged between 10 and 13....The commission was established by Catholic bishops in France at the end of 2018 to shed light on abuses and restore public confidence in the church." *9 Tangi Salaun, Ingrid Melander

Given the secretive, privileged, and powerful patriarchal culture among the clerical class, is there any reason to think that these abuses don't go back much farther in history?

Another example:
"Leaders in the Southern Baptist Convention [U.S.A.] on [5-22-2022] released a major third-party investigation that found that sexual abuse survivors often were ignored, minimized and 'even vilified' by top clergy in the nation's largest Protestant denomination. The...report includes shocking details about specific cases and shines a light on how denominational leaders for decades actively resisted calls for abuse prevention....Jennifer Lyell, a survivor...once was the highest-paid woman executive at the SBC and [her] story of sexual abuse at a Southern Baptist seminary is detailed in the report. 'This is a denomination [that] is through and through about power.' The report also names several senior church leaders who protected alleged abusers, including three past presidents of the convention." *10 Sarah Pulliam Bailey

Not only are the abuses horrible but high-level cover-ups compound the crimes.

Long-standing patriarchal religious traditions abound all over the world. So-called "temporary marriages " add to male privileges while disadvantaging females in a patriarchal society.

"'Mutaa,' a 1,400-year old tradition alternately known as pleasure marriage and temporary marriage, is regaining popularity among Iraq's majority Shiite Muslim population....According to Shiite religious law, unmarried women may enter into pleasure marriages with men (married or not) for periods as brief as a few minutes or as long as a lifetime....Shiite clerics, including Iraq's highest religious authority, Grand Ayatollah Ali Sistani, have sanctioned mutaa....Some Shiite scholars say the prophet Muhammad sanctioned mutaa marriages for his companions during their wars and campaigns to spread Islam in present-day Saudi Arabia. Other historians argue that the practice existed in pre-Islamic societies and was later permitted by Muhammad....[In] the Shiite theocratic state of Iran...mutaa is even more popular." *11 Solomon Moore

Another patriarchal religious tradition facilitates child-marriages and involves "forced conversion."

"[N]early 1,000 girls from religious minorities...are forced to convert to Islam in Pakistan each year, largely to pave the way for marriages that are under the legal age and nonconsensual....The U.S. Sate Department this month [December 2020] declared Pakistan 'a country of particular concern' for violations of religious freedoms....The declaration was based in part on an appraisal by the U.S. Commission on International Religious Freedom that underage girls in the minority Hindu, Christian, and Sikh communities were 'kidnapped for forced conversion to Islam, forcibly married and subjected to rape'....Forced conversions thrive unchecked on a moneymaking web that involves Islamic clerics who solemnize the marriages, magistrates who legalize the unions and corrupt local police who aid the culprits by refusing to investigate or sabotaging investigations, say child protection activists." *12 Kathy Gannon

Patriarchal institutional religion, regardless of the religion, enhances male privileges and puts girls and women, in particular, in a more subordinate and vulnerable position, subject to ongoing abuses.

<u>Jesus and the Discipleship/Liberation Movement</u>

So, what is God's next move in the struggle to bring salvation, justice, and liberation to the whole world and to overcome Patriarchy? It may well be that the time is ripe for a holistic re-forming of Jesus' discipleship/liberation movement. Based on all that has occurred in the past century it may well be time for Jesus' movement to re-emerge. Of course, for this to occur Jesus needs a lot more followers and disciples. Organizing small groups, households, and small communities is needed.

Every generation needs to rediscover Jesus—and to discard all the noise, bad theology, and bad Christian witness that surrounds him. Patriarchal institutional Christianity makes it difficult for Jesus' movement to regain traction.

To become full partners with Jesus means joining Jesus' movement and working to overcome patriarchal fragmentation and to "restore the whole." In all times, to be holistic Jesus' liberation movement must be radically "feminist"—in the sense that it must be completely against the reign of Patriarchy on Earth. Part of this is recognizing that patriarchal institutional religion is inherently fragmenting and oppressive and thus needs to be stepped away from. Small group discipleship formation is needed. *Really, Patriarchy has no other serious challenger to overcome it. None at all!* The only true hope for saving humanity and the world and overcoming Patriarchy is through Jesus' holistic discipleship/liberation movement. This is the plight of the Earth. Patriarchy rules human civilizations and there is only one true hope for overcoming it.

The struggle for universal liberation and to overcome Patriarchy will be both very rewarding and quite costly. History shows that Patriarchy has enduring power, adaptability, and resiliency and will not go down without a hell of a fight. Followers of Jesus will need a lot of discipleship preparation and training for a long struggle and should not look for a quick and easy victory.

> "Then Jesus began to say to them, 'Beware that no one leads you astray. Many will come in my name and say, 'I am he!' and they will lead many astray. When you hear of wars and rumors of wars, do not be alarmed; this must take place, but the end is still to come. For nation will rise against nation, and kingdom against kingdom; there will be earthquakes in various places; there will be famines. *This is but the beginning of the birthpangs*." (Mark 13:5-8)

As Gramsci once said, "*The old world is dying but the new refuses to be born.*" How long will it take? The length of time depends upon humanity's free will decisions—and on discipleship to Jesus and reliance on love, nonviolence, and God's Spirit-power.

Footnotes

1. Mary Daly, Gyn/Ecology: The Metaethics of Radical Feminism, Beacon Press, Boston, 1978, p. 39.
2. John F. Haught, Resting on the Future: Catholic Theology for an Unfinished Universe, Bloomsbury, New York, 2015, pp. 95,98,99.
3. What some people want is cheap forgiveness, cheap grace, and a cheap blessing of their lifestyle. They can get all these things by going to a church service and then leave the church service feeling justified/righteous. A little spiritual whitewashing can make one feel good. And then people can get into their cars which fill the church parking lot and get on with their lives in the patriarchal society.
4. Elisabeth Schussler Fiorenza, In Memory of Her: A Feminist Theological Reconstruction of Christian Origins, Crossroad, New York, 1983, pp. 286-287.
5. Elisabeth Schussler Fiorenza, p. 253.
6. William Durland, God or Nations: Radical Theology for the Religious Peace Movement, Fortkamp, Baltimore, Maryland, 1989, pp. 99,118.
7. It seems to me that there is a high likelihood that the Gospel of Mark was written by a woman.
8. Walter Klassen, "Anabaptism: Neither Catholic Nor Protestant," Christian History, Volume IV, No. 1, 1985, p. 34.
9. Tangi Salaun, Ingrid Melander, Reuters, "French report details abuse," Duluth News Tribune, October 6, 2021.
10. Sarah Pulliam Bailey, Washington Post, "Probe finds Southern Baptists ignored years of sex abuse," Star Tribune, May 23, 2022.
11. Solomon Moore, LA Times, "'Mutaa' marriages make comeback," Duluth News Tribune, January 15, 2006.
12. Kathy Gannon, AP, "Pakistani girls forcibly converted to Islam to marry older men," Star Tribune, December 29, 2020.

Chapter 9

The Alpha and the Omega

> "'I am the Alpha and the Omega', says the Lord God, who is and who was and who is to come, the Almighty." (Revelation 1:8)
>
> "And the one who was seated on the throne said, 'See, I am making all things new'....'I am the Alpha and the Omega, the beginning and the end.'" (Revelation 21:5-6)

God is the Alpha and the Omega. And since Jesus, the Son of God, and God are one, Jesus can also be identified as the Alpha and the Omega, the beginning and the end. God/Jesus is the starting or beginning point of all creation. And all creation is destined to move toward the "end" or ultimate goal of God/Jesus.

> "...our being the chapter in nature's history when the universe (or multiverse) has finally begun to open itself consciously, prayerfully, and gratefully to the coming of God, the absolute future, the goal (and not just the originator) of all creation....Our sense of self-worth, therefore, is understandably felt most fully in moments of hope, that is, in our heightened capacity for anticipating the coming of God into a creation that has always been a story of awakening to its future. The soul that longs for God 'as the deer longs for streams of fresh water' (Psa. 42:1) has the function of bringing to conscious expression the anticipatory leaning of all creation, no matter how broadly construed, in its journey into God." *1 John F. Haught

What God/Jesus has started with creation, God/Jesus will bring toward creation's ultimate destination, with a little help from their friends.

The destiny of creation is to move ever closer to the Omega, to the ultimate goal of wholeness and oneness with God. Evolution is long and slow but it is characterized by progress. Evolutionary progress is not mechanistic and "deterministic." Evolutionary progress is never in a straight line. It is always variable, with ebbs and flows. It incorporates humanity's free will and freedom to make choices with different consequences. It allows for Patriarchy to do great evil. However, God's greatest intervention into patriarchal history—the sending of Jesus the Messiah—gives assurance of humanity's ultimate destiny. The pivotal sending of Jesus provides essential help for humanity to make a major course correction. But because of humanity's free will and the power of Patriarchy, the path forward is full of setbacks. Even so the sending of Jesus tips the balance, is just enough to seal the deal, and ultimately sends humanity—and nature and Earth and the cosmos—forward into the future towards the Omega. No matter how terrible and miserable Patriarchy makes life on Earth, eventually a lot of people will choose to become partners with Jesus, will follow Jesus on the path of love and nonviolence, and will work to turn the tide.

For humanity, and for the world, there is only one true hope for overcoming Patriarchy and bringing about universal salvation, justice, and liberation. But one true hope is enough. The one true hope comes through Jesus and his discipleship/liberation movement. The one true hope is a sure hope—it is a certain hope—because it is based on a divine-human partnership with a God of infinite love and infinite Spirit-power. And so the lifelong journey of discipleship to Jesus, despite the hardships, is always a life and a journey of great hope for transforming the world. Followers of Jesus have the responsibility for bearing this hope and keeping it in the forefront of their minds.

The major obstacle and problem, of course, is Patriarchy. In chapter 8 we saw how patriarchal institutional religion presented God/Jesus with a myriad of difficulties for re-forming and advancing Jesus' holistic movement. What will be examined here is the problem of patriarchal societies being swayed towards atheism and secularism. The denial of the existence of God means turning away from the only true hope for humanity and the world. It means pushing the fulfillment of this hope further into the future. It delays the advancement of Jesus' liberation movement and prolongs the reign of Patriarchy on Earth, with devastating consequences.

An intellectual case for atheism has been developed by scientists and philosophers stemming from a patriarchal mindset, contemporary cosmology, and the groundbreaking work of Charles Darwin and his book *On the Origin of Species*. The historical development of nature and all life are all connected together and occurred over a very long time. Homo sapiens are a part of that long developmental process and not an exception to it. Innumerable valuable insights about nature and life have been revealed through evolutionary biology. The problem of distorting and mis-interpreting these insights comes from *overlaying* these insights with an *atheist and materialist belief-system*. It is *the combination of evolutionary biology and contemporary cosmology with atheistic materialism* that can lead people away from integrating scientific knowledge with faith in a God of creation, liberation, and eternal life.

The scientific insights of evolutionary biology are expanded upon by scientific atheists to develop a materialist belief-system (which can also be called "evolutionary materialism or naturalism"). This materialist belief-system purportedly can explain "everything" and yet it completely eliminates the God who created and rules the universe.

> "'Evolutionary naturalism,' as we may label this relatively new but confident creed, claims that natural selection of random adaptive changes in organisms over an immense period of time can account in an ultimate way for all living and behavioral traits, including human intelligence, moral aspiration, and religious longing....The impersonal evolutionary engine of creation is said to be powered by three mindless ingredients: accidental organic variations (now understood to be caused mostly by genetic mutations), blind natural selection of heritable traits, and an enormous amount of time. This simple three-part Darwinian recipe, according to the evolutionary naturalists can account all by itself for *every* aspect of life." *2 John F. Haught

Similarly, the scientific insights of contemporary cosmology, beginning with the "Big Bang" origin of the universe 13.8 billion years ago, are expanded upon by scientific atheists to further enhance their materialist belief-system. By looking back at the distant past, at how the universe originated and developed over billions of years, scientific atheists believe they can both accurately explain all life in the present and even predict, with certainty, the demise of the entire universe in the distant future.

> "This archaeological mode of inquiry typically assumes that the appropriate way to comprehend the world is by breaking down present complexity into its simpler

elements. In the context of Big Bang cosmology, the intellectual and experimental decomposition of complex entities into their elementary constituents is simultaneously a journey into the far distant past. Scientific analysis follows the cosmic trail back to an epoch when the universe existed only as dispersed subatomic units....In this intellectual setting, the universe is not a narrative but instead an aimless movement of mindless material stuff across vast periods of time." *3 John F. Haught

An atheistic and materialist belief-system sees only a truncated version of "the whole." It eliminates any real deity, rejects a "spiritual realm" of life, belittles or minimizes the universe's undeniable movement towards life, more complexity, more biodiversity, more "being," more mind/intuition/ consciousness, more of God's and Jesus' involvement in liberation history, and eliminates hope for the long-term future. It peers into the remote past and sees lots of random particles upon which to base its deadening philosophy.

"A materialistic metaphysics of the past, then, is in effect an 'ontology of death' in which lifelessness is primary, and life secondary, epiphenomenal, and, hence, not 'really real'....What is objectionable, then, is not analytical science as such but the atomistic philosophical mentality...that reduces all of nature to protons, quarks, leptons, fermion, bosons, and so on....It is an all-encompassing vision of reality...leading our minds downward and backward into an atomic mist." *4 John F. Haught

By focusing on "the little pieces" an atheistic and materialist belief-system fails to see "the whole."

An atheistic and materialist belief-system has been criticized by some as being essentially an "ontology of death." The creator God and the preeminence of life are squeezed out of this narrow-minded picture of "reality." An atheistic and materialist belief-system looks at the origin of the universe and claims that the origin was completely lifeless. It was akin to a "state of death"—being lifeless, mindless, and without purpose or meaning. Then, the presumption is that most of the history of the universe's 13.8 billion years were also lifeless and without purpose. Only about 3.8 billion years ago did life arise on Earth. And even in this "Goldilocks region" of our solar system where life can flourish, a materialist belief-system views death as preeminent. Death, not life, could be described as the superior characteristic of nature. For the evolution of life, death is essential for natural selection to occur. All organisms must die in order for better hereditary traits to gradually prevail in new organisms. And even for the most complex and developed creatures—human beings—an atheistic and materialist belief-system believes that death has the final word over life.

"Cosmic pessimism [a.k.a. atheistic materialism] ... considers all loss, including the death of human persons, permanent and final. Science, it claims, has now ruled out the possibility of any subjective survival of death. Since our own consciousness is a function of how our material brains are organized, when this organization disintegrates, so does the capacity for thought. Not only our personal lives but also everything else that has ever occurred in the universe will come to rest in a state of total unconsciousness in the end." *5 John F. Haught
Proponents of an atheistic and materialist belief-system fervently believe they have acquired sufficient knowledge of everything to accurately predict the distant future outcome of the entire universe. The prediction, of course, is of a completely dead universe, where energy exhaustion has brought a permanent end to all life. In this belief-system death will reign and there will be no memory of anything. All striving for whatever purpose will end in futility and lifelessness. This deadening "ontology of death" belief-system offers no lasting hope for humanity and for the world.

An atheistic and materialist belief-system is yet another philosophical branch of Patriarchy. Patriarchy is leading humanity down the path of "death and destruction." Patriarchy deceptively leads people to choose a path that leads to more death, and not more life. Patriarchy "fragments the whole," breaking the whole into pieces, and creates divisions. Patriarchy tends to separate humans from God and from nature and from each other. Patriarchy also breaks down an individual's natural constituency of spirit, mind, and body, which is rooted in nature. Patriarchy undermines God's work to move humanity and nature forward towards greater liberation, unity, and fulfillment.

So it needs to be continuously affirmed that humans have deep interconnections with God, nature, and spiritual life. Humans are not a mindless and random product of evolution—

but are an incredibly important species for moving nature, Earth, and the universe forward in purposeful evolutionary progress. And while Patriarchy works to break things down and is leading the world into Earth's 6th great age of mass extinctions of species, the living God is working to draw life towards a new wholeness, a new unity, and a New Creation—drawing life in the direction of Godself, the Omega. God is pitted against Patriarchy. And the way of discipleship to Jesus polarizes as people can choose between "two poles"—either Jesus or Patriarchy. Life or Death. Jesus/God are against an atheistic and materialist belief-system that purports to see "the whole" but actually fails terribly to see the big story of variable but ultimately purposeful and never-ending evolutionary progress toward the Omega.

Atheism is only one of Patriarchy's many contributors to secularism. Secularism finds support from most patriarchal institutions. Secularism abounds through capitalist businesses and workplaces, governments, criminal legal systems, gangs, affluent lifestyles, consumerism, popular entertainment, public education, various organizations, etc. A secularist lifestyle eliminates God from most, if not all, aspects of life. When even "people of faith" lead a mostly secularist lifestyle they are giving witness to the public-at-large that God is mostly irrelevant to their lives. That is a problem. It reinforces the pervasiveness of patriarchal culture and society and it shows that Patriarchy continues to "win on the ground."

Secularism can lead people on many paths that provide false hopes for overcoming Patriarchy, saving humanity, and saving the world. One path, currently quite popular, is to work to build so-called "democracy" all over the world. As I have written previously a lot about the myths of democracy I will just briefly mention this false path to social justice.

All governments, including so-called "democratic governments," represent organized dominative power and organized violence, i.e., police and military forces that support unjust patriarchal social orders. "Democratic" governments, based on dominative power, coercion, and violence, create and support political and social hierarchies. Hence they support inequality and injustice. They support a patriarchal "domination system." All governments provide a false model of "justice" through their criminal legal systems. The true nature of criminal legal systems is best revealed by the crude, physical violence of police forces acting in the interests of the ruling class—and by the crushing oppression of jails, prisons, fines, and probation which mostly target poor people and minorities. So-called "democratic government" is just a "brilliant" (from the perspective of the ruling class) historical mutation of patriarchal governance that fools large numbers of people into supporting it. All governments based on dominative power, violence, and social hierarchies are inimical to true social justice. They do not offer a true path for overcoming Patriarchy. They only offer paths for getting further enmeshed into Patriarchy.

Secular grassroots movements "of the people" also offer false paths and false hopes for overcoming Patriarchy. In theory, popular people-movements can dismantle Patriarchy and build something better. However, this theory is not based on a key big-picture context. In the big-picture context of a very broad understanding of Patriarchy, this theory unravels. Patriarchy is a behemoth—it is a "social totality." Since all people are immersed in patriarchal cultures and societies from their births, Patriarchy has deep roots in all people. In secular grassroots movements with radical aims, these deep roots will come to the forefront and create divisions. A secular people's movement will be riddled with internal contradictions within individuals and within the movement. With imperfect human leadership it will lack clarity of vision and strategies. It will eventually coalesce around reformist positions or try, and fail, to represent something "new and different." In the end Patriarchy will prevail. In practice, in reality, people, by themselves, will never overcome Patriarchy. People need a divine partner and leader, ongoing personal transformation, the forming of a spirit-mind-body harmony, and the benefits of Spirit-power. Hence, people need Jesus/God to overcome Patriarchy; Jesus needs a lot more followers and disciples to overcome Patriarchy.

Atheism and secularism, by their exclusion of God and blindness toward the spiritual realm of life, can only offer false paths and false hopes for overcoming Patriarchy. Atheism and secularism support patriarchal fragmentation. Atheism and secularism make impossible the forming within people of a spirit-mind-body whole. They are branches of Patriarchy. They are like a weight that depresses and holds down the human spirit and supports divisions among humanity. In contrast to this, Jesus and his discipleship/liberation movement offer a hope-filled path on which the human spirit can rise to new heights. It is a path of moving towards wholeness—with a new Jesus-centered family and community—which restores connections with wider humanity, other living creatures, nature, the Earth, and the cosmos.

The human spirit is meant to soar. If the human spirit is not soaring it is because some aspect or aspects of Patriarchy are weighing it down, perhaps crushing it, and hiding the path that leads to God and wholeness. Human beings are physical beings, sexual beings, social beings, *and spiritual beings*. (Human beings can also be described as intelligent beings— however, I don't want to go into that frustrating topic.) The basic constituency of a person is a blend of spirit, mind, and body that is rooted in nature. The physical body's lifespan is relatively "short-lived" and our bodies will eventually wear out and die. But humans' spiritual being ("soul") is long-lasting and lives on after the physical body dies. So human beings are essentially spiritual beings since that which is long-lasting is more essential than that which is relatively short-lived. Basically, we are souls, we are spiritual beings and the spirit of life within us comes from God.

The apostle Paul wrote of the physical body being the "temple" for God's Spirit.
"Or do you not know that your body is a temple of the Holy Spirit within you....therefore glorify God in your body." (1 Corinthians 6:19-20)
While living on Earth our souls are fully integrated with a physical body. Upon the death of the physical body our souls, with full consciousness, continue to live on in a spiritual realm—and yet are still connected to nature and material life on Earth. The physical and spiritual realms are blended together in mysterious ways (and not subject to scientific scrutiny). The spiritual realm is not a completely separate (fragmented or divided) realm. The physical and spiritual realms are connected and united in ways not well understood (although some Native and indigenous peoples grasped this—and Christians can believe in both the immanence and transcendence of God/Spirit).

We are souls, and before God all souls are equal regardless of the physical body, male or female or mixed, that our souls inhabit. Since God is the Alpha and the Omega, the creator, liberator, and giver of eternal life, we may realize that we are meant to be drawn, through the eternity of time, ever closer to God, the Omega. God is the goal and completion of our souls.

We are meant to be drawn, with all creation, ever deeper into a oneness with God.

The human spirit is meant to soar. Jesus calls people to follow him and to become part of a divine-human partnership in the struggle to overcome Patriarchy and to work for a New Creation. The path of following Jesus can be hard and costly. It involves daily self-discipline and the uprooting of all the desires of living in an affluent, consumerist, patriarchal society. But it brings us into a closer relationship with Jesus and benefits humanity, the Earth, and the universe (since all things are connected). Jesus is the Messiah, the Son of God, the incarnation of God, and Jesus and God are one. If you want to know God better, then get to know Jesus better. Jesus reveals who God is. And Jesus is totally awesome. Of course, God is also totally awesome. In truth, God is mind-bogglingly awesome. God is love. God is infinite love. God is perfect love. To follow Jesus closely is to be drawn into the stream of God's Spirit, God's will. And God's will is based on perfect love, infinite knowledge, and total wisdom. This is the path that lifts up the human spirit—and, in time, all of creation.

The human spirit is meant to soar. As spiritual beings, as souls, human beings have a natural longing to know God. Of course, this human longing for God often has been misdirected through patriarchal institutional religion. Worship of God, bringing a closer spiritual communion of people with God, has long been distorted by powerful patriarchal religious leaders and institutions. In a conversation with an outcast Samaritan ("mixed-blood") woman, Jesus, the Messiah, reveals to her the need for a changing social order and for a rejection of patriarchal worship traditions.

> "The woman said to him, 'Sir, I see that you are a prophet. Our ancestors worshiped on this mountain, but you say that the place where people must worship is in Jerusalem.' Jesus said to her, 'Woman, believe me, the hour is coming when you will worship the [Father/Mother] neither on this mountain nor in Jerusalem....God is spirit and those who worship [God] must worship in spirit and truth.'" (John 4:19-21,24)

To worship God holistically "in spirit and truth" worship must: 1. be centered specifically around Jesus, the divine leader of God's liberation movement, who is working to bring liberation and wholeness to all humanity and creation; 2. be opposed to

Patriarchy in its many oppressive forms including patriarchal religious buildings and institutions, a clerical class of clergy and priests, exclusively male God-language, patriarchal theology and ideology, patriarchal dress codes, creeds, hymns, rituals, etc.; and 3. be open to charismatic gifts of the Spirit and be open to spontaneity in word or song or movement or dance. Worship in spirit and truth is as beneficial for the health of the soul as is food and water for the body. Worship in spirit and truth helps to bring about spirit-mind-body harmony. Worship in spirit and truth uplifts the human spirit and can result in a radiant joy which can be carried over into the daily struggle against Patriarchy.

The human spirit is meant to soar. Presently, however, Patriarchy continues to rule human civilizations and to inflict devastating damage. Jesus and the discipleship/liberation movement will eventually overcome Patriarchy. Victory is certain. But it will take *some time* because Jesus needs *a lot more* followers and disciples....The path of discipleship to Jesus can lead one to deeper levels of faith and consciousness of God's presence and awesomeness....More of Jesus in one's life means more love and joy....And, well, surely we all can add to this.

> "See, I am coming soon; my reward is with me, to repay according to everyone's work. I am the Alpha and the Omega, the first and the last, the beginning and the end." (Revelation 22:12-13)

Footnotes

1. John F. Haught, <u>Resting on the Future: Catholic Theology for an Unfinished Universe</u>, Bloomsbury, 2015, p. 112.
2. John F. Haught, p. 55.
3. John F. Haught, p. 59.
4. John F. Haught, pp. 24-25.
5. John F. Haught, p. 115.